Contents

Supporting Struggling Writers in the Elementary Classroom

University of Minnesota, Twin Cities
Minneapolis, Minnesota, USA
and Hamline University
St. Paul, Minnesota, USA

UNIVERSITY COLLEGE CHICHESTER LIBRARIES

AUTHOR:	WS 2192592 5
TITLE:	CLASS No: 372. 6 CHR
DATE: 12/02.	SUBJECT: TED.

INTERNATIONAL Reading Association

800 Barksdale Road, PO Box 8139
Newark, Delaware 19714-8139, USA
www.reading.org

The International Reading Association attempts, through its publications, to provide a forum for a wide spectrum of opinions on reading. This policy permits divergent viewpoints without implying the endorsement of the Association.

Director of Publications   Joan M. Irwin
Editorial Director, Books and Special Projects   Matthew W. Baker
Senior Editor, Books and Special Projects   Tori Mello Bachman
Permissions Editor   Janet S. Parrack
Production Editor   Shannon Benner
Assistant Editor   Corinne M. Mooney
Editorial Assistant   Tyanna L. Collins
Publications Manager   Beth Doughty
Production Department Manager   Iona Sauscermen
Supervisor, Electronic Publishing   Anette Schütz
Senior Electronic Publishing Specialist   Cheryl J. Strum
Electronic Publishing Specialist   R. Lynn Harrison
Proofreader   Charlene M. Nichols

Project Editor   Tori Mello Bachman

Cover Photo   PhotoDisc

Copyright 2002 by the International Reading Association, Inc.

Library of Congress Cataloging-in-Publication Data
Christenson, Teresa A.
Supporting struggling writers in the elementary classroom / Teresa A. Christenson.
      p. cm.—(Kids InSight series)
Includes bibliographical references and index.
   ISBN 0-87207-447-1
1. English language—Composition and exercises—Study and teaching (Elementary) 2. Language arts (Elementary) I. Title. II. Series.
LB1576 .D5562 2002
372.62'3—dc21
                                                                    2002002892

This book is dedicated to
Kenda, Paulo, Daniel, Amy,
and their teacher, Kate.

Note From the Series Editor

It is a pleasure to introduce readers to Teresa A. Christenson and the fifth-grade students that she describes in this book. Teresa shares stories about the experiences of four struggling writers and their teacher, Kate, as well as her own one-on-one work with the student writers. Through careful description and analysis, we see an excellent teacher who strives to use a writing workshop approach that includes an important focus on skills and strategy work with individual students. Teresa shares information about how Kate set up her classroom to support all learners; the strategies she used to support struggling writers; and examples of lessons that worked, some that did not, and why. We are not presented with an endorsement of a particular approach, but instead we see a careful discussion of how to adapt an approach to make it work for children who experience difficulties as they write.

It is also important to note that Teresa chose to write this book because of her own experiences with her daughter, who was diagnosed as having a writing disability. Teresa spent many hours with teachers and specialists to understand her daughter's learning challenges and how to advocate for quality teaching and learning experiences. As she comments, it is often through our own personal experiences and struggles that we determine the focus for our professional lives and work. Thus, Teresa brings great knowledge and passion to the writing of this book, and I am pleased that her book has been selected by a respected panel of literacy experts to be published in the Kids InSight (KI) series. I believe this book makes a tremendous contribution to the field of intermediate-grade elementary students' literacy.

The KI series provides practical information for K–12 teachers and brings to the fore stories about—and the voices of—children and adolescents as the basis for instructional decisions. Books in the series are designed to encourage educators to address the challenge of meeting the literacy needs of all students as individuals and learners in and out of our classrooms, while recognizing that there are no easy answers or quick fixes to achieving this goal. Sociocultural perspectives of how students learn are the foundation of each KI book, and authors address learners' emotional, affective, and cognitive development. Dialoguing with other professionals, reading research findings in literacy and education in general, inquiring into teaching and learning processes, observing as well as talking and listening to students, documenting successful practices, and reflecting on literacy events using writing and analysis are strategies and actions embraced by teachers described in KI books. Authors of these books allow us to see into classrooms or view students' lives outside of school in order to learn about the thoughts and dreams of young people, as well as the goals and planning processes of teachers. Finally, we are privy to how events actually unfold during formal and informal lessons— the successful and the less-than-successful moments—through the use of transcripts and interview comments woven throughout KI books.

In *Supporting Struggling Writers in the Elementary Classroom*, Teresa shares how she worked to keep kids *in sight* as she observed and wrote about particular students as they engaged in various writing activities. For example, Teresa studied the strategies used to support struggling writers. She examined how individual writers used particular strategies and what happened when knowledgeable teachers intervened at appropriate moments to help students shift their own learning in effective ways. In this book, Teresa also allows us to see the developmental writing processes that Kenda, Paulo, Daniel, and Amy went through and indicators of their growth along the way. Specifically, she shows us writing samples from across the year from the four learners. This careful documentation and analysis of students' work, coupled with understanding the lesson goals and the interventions that occurred to support the writers as they worked on various projects, enables us to see strategy work and learning in practice. Even more important, Teresa makes the point that the talk between teachers and students as they engage in lessons is key to students' learning. Learning to listen to students, knowing what to say and when to "nudge them forward," and seeking to let them lead the conversation are all key to effective teaching and learning experiences.

At the heart of the book is the support Teresa offers us as teachers through her analyses and reflections after working with individual students.

For example, Teresa tells us about the writing activities and lessons students are asked to complete. She then describes for us what strategies the learner used, documents when a teacher stepped in and supported the student through instruction using modeling or scaffolding or explicit directions, shows how students modified strategies to make them work in particular situations, and displays the students' work after these interactions. We also are privy to the reflective comments made by the teacher after the learning event. This key information allows us to think alongside a teacher as she reconsiders what the students' actions were, what she did, what worked and did not and why, and what opportunities should be designed to support the students' future growth. I particularly like the way Teresa poses questions for herself such as, "I wonder what happened when Kenda tried to take the strategy we had talked about but ended up with a modified tool that served her in some ways but not in others as she wrote her story?" It is through question posing that we, as teachers, continue to examine what is happening in our classrooms and with individual students. In addition, Teresa offers a wealth of information from the research literature about writing processes and strategies. This information is carefully placed throughout the book to allow readers to address tensions encountered as they look closely at students' work and teaching and learning practices.

In her book, Teresa allows learners to show us what they have understood, what they feel, and how they will use the knowledge and ideas they have learned to empower themselves as intermediate-grade learners. We see students who initially only saw their weaknesses as writers but who eventually see and call upon their personal strengths and learning strategies. Teresa reminds us that teacher support for struggling writers takes many forms: working directly with learners to solve problems, empowering students with effective and flexible strategies, motivating learners each day in whatever ways they need our support, and enlisting parents as advocates and allies in the learning process. Finally, Teresa tells us that as she worked in Kate's classroom she learned how to pay attention to learners like Kenda, Paulo, Daniel, and Amy and sought to see them as her teachers. This focus allows us to develop insights about intermediate grade-level learners.

Deborah R. Dillon
Series Editor
University of Minnesota, Twin Cities
Minneapolis, Minnesota, USA

Kids InSight Review Board

Jan Turbill
University of Wollongong
Wollongong, New South Wales,
  Australia

Angela Ward
University of Saskatchewan
Saskatoon, Saskatchewan,
  Canada

Deborah A. Wooten
Glenwood Landing School
Glen Head, New York, USA

Josephine P. Young
Arizona State University
Tempe, Arizona, USA

Acknowledgments

There is an African proverb that states "it takes a village to raise a child." Throughout the writing of this book, I have come to learn that it also takes a village to support the work of a single author. There are many people who have encouraged and guided my efforts.

I could not have written this book without the background provided to me by the Education faculty at the University of Saskatchewan (Saskatoon, Saskatchewan, Canada). Each instructor challenged me to step beyond my comfort boundaries and stretch my thinking in new ways. Dr. Angela Ward, an exceptional scholar, guided my work as a graduate student. Her mentoring played a pivotal role in the direction of my career, and she continues to be a source of support for me. Dr. Sam Robinson led me into the area of writing and provided the encouragement I needed for the creation of this book. His teaching is deeply woven into my thinking and will surface throughout the following pages.

I also would like to express my gratitude to those individuals associated with the development of the Kids InSight series. Dr. Deborah Dillon, editor of the series, provided invaluable feedback throughout the process of writing. Deborah's encouragement and positive approach helped to fuel my work from start to finish. A special thanks to the anonymous reviewers who prepared important feedback to my writing and provided me with a vision for improving the manuscript. I was also blessed with superb editors from IRA—Tori Bachman, Matt Baker, and everyone in the Books Department. I thank each of you for the care with which you read the manuscript and the thoughtfulness in your responses. You each helped to make this book better than it would have been had I written it alone.

I am grateful, too, for the support of my family. It was my parents, Bill and Kay Harter, who first demonstrated for me the value of teaching and learning. All that I do now relies on the solid foundation they provided during my childhood. They have shaped my life and provided years of positive influence. My own two children, Benjamin and Jenna, graciously supported my time at the computer and provided the smiles I needed when I emerged from my writing. Thank you for the basketball games, the Saturday night movies, the bike rides, the laughter, and the energy you have brought to our home. All have called me away from my work and reenergized my writing. Most of all, I thank my husband and very best friend, Randy. His contributions to my work have extended far beyond my years as a graduate student.

The dedication of this book suggests the gratitude I feel toward fifth-grade teacher Kate and her classroom of writers. The voices of Kenda, Paulo, Daniel, and Amy will be heard throughout the pages of this book. These students became my teachers, trusting me with their thoughts and showing me what it means to be young student writers. Kate welcomed me into her classroom. It was a privilege to teach and learn side by side with this caring and knowledgeable educator. Kate's never-ending support and guidance contributed significantly to the foundation upon which my ideals for the teaching of writing have been built. I will be forever grateful.

Chapter 1

Learning From the Children We Teach

> Ms. C.:   *Do you like writing, Kenda?*
>
> Kenda: *Yes. But I have problems...like trying to get it all on a sheet, 'cuz I can think like a storm...but I can't get it down on a piece of paper. That is what is really hard sometimes. And well, sometimes it is just like, "Oh, I can't think! I can't think!" And then I just...it feels really weird in there and I try and think. I try and think and then I can never think for the longest time.*

This quote from a fifth-grade student reminds me of the difficulties faced by young writers. There are many frustrations and obstacles that come with learning to write. Writing is not an easy task. Finding the right words for ideas can at times be a difficult and time-consuming process. Murray (1984) describes the process of writing as "one of the most complicated human activities" (p. 6). Every writer will, at one time or another, struggle with this complex process. Struggling is an important part of learning to write for everyone.

If *all* writers occasionally find the writing process complicated, what makes struggling writers different from other writers? How are their written products different? How is their writing process different? What are their specific struggles? Kenda's story, together with the stories of three other students in a fifth-grade writing workshop, taught me a tremendous amount about what it means to be a young writer. This book shares the writing journey of these four learners and documents their doubts, fears, and triumphs as they learn to write.

Reflection Point 1.1 _____

1. I encourage you to obtain a journal where you can record your thoughts as you read and reflect on the ideas found in this book. Begin by describing your personal journey of learning to write. What memories surface when you think of learning to write in elementary school? Did these memories leave a positive or negative impression?

2. What home experiences influenced your abilities as a writer? What role has writing played in your past? What recent experiences have you had writing? How will these experiences come with you into the classroom?

Who Are the Students in This Book?

Four young students welcomed me into their writing classroom and helped me learn from their experiences. During the time I spent with these students, I learned how to pay attention to children and think more clearly about what should be happening in the writing classroom. I sharpened my observational skills and learned how informative children can be when we take the time to listen—really listen. I have recognized that I can learn about my teaching by listening to their stories of learning.

Throughout this book, I use the authentic dialogue and language of the students. Significant moments in the classroom have been captured and shared through discussion. Student writing samples have been preserved and represented to provide insight into student thinking, and pseudonyms have been used to assure confidentiality. With this in mind, I will introduce you to four young writers: Kenda, Paulo, Daniel, and Amy.

Each brought their own unique personality, strengths, and learning needs to the classroom.

Kenda

Kenda, whose voice is represented in this chapter's opening quote, arrived at school as a transient student, bringing with her learning experiences from four other elementary settings. She was an independent young girl, riding two city buses by herself to get to school each day. Kenda recently had moved into the community to live with her mother. Her previous experiences as a student in various school environments had been challenging. It was easy for everyone to be attracted to this kind, sensitive, and courageous personality.

Kenda's interests were in fashion design. I vividly recall a fashion design book she once created. The first page of her book began with detail: colorful shirts, fashionable pants, and models drawn with specific features. Kenda's writing in the classroom did not reflect such detail, though. Here she struggled to remain focused on written tasks and found the physical and mechanical aspects of writing to be tedious and time consuming. Kenda worked best when I sat alongside her desk, guiding her attention and refocusing her energies. In our conversations, Kenda's language tended to focus on her learning difficulties and insecurities. A self-awareness of her personal strengths and learning abilities seemed to be missing.

Paulo

Dark hair and large brown eyes framed Paulo's captivating face. He happened to sit very near me as each writing class began. Our close proximity meant we regularly exchanged quick glances and grins. During class time, Paulo hesitated to get personally involved in his work, and he needed regular encouragement to complete assignments. Paulo kept his writing utensils around him but rarely wrote unless asked to do so by the teacher. When his teacher made this request, Paulo was slow to start writing. He struggled to settle on a writing topic of interest. Paulo's body language frequently reflected disinterest. He often appeared bored, complaining that his hand was sore or his pinkie finger hurt. As time passed, the classroom teacher and I learned that Paulo thrived on positive comments and small words of encouragement. His success was driven by the thoughts of others, and affirmation was critical to his development. Paulo's mother was highly supportive and regularly involved in school and classroom activities, and she guided him through many homework assignments. She wanted Paulo to experience success in school and was willing to devote a tremendous amount of time to supporting his growth.

Daniel

Daniel was Paulo's best buddy. The two of them, along with a third friend, were inseparable. Daniel came from a supportive home environment. His parents were in tune with Daniel's abilities, and they regularly looked for ways at home to support his development. Daniel's personality quietly melded into the busy classroom. With the hustle of activity that surrounds fifth-grade students, it would have been easy to overlook Daniel's needs. Daniel quickly got to work after each recess, and he worked hard each day. He was a diligent, quiet worker, always focused with his head down and his pencil in motion. In the writing classroom, Daniel especially struggled with the mechanics of writing, primarily spelling, capitalization, and punctuation.

Amy

Amy was one of the first young writers I met when I entered this classroom. That first day, she confidently approached me with a large smile and energetic voice. "What is your name? Why are you here?" she asked. Her genuine interest in my role created a welcoming atmosphere in the classroom. As time passed, Amy continued to greet me each day with interesting conversations, stories to tell, and experiences to share. Amy's teacher and I observed how Amy's interactions in the classroom were heavily influenced by the thoughts of her peers. It was important for her to be accepted in the social circle and remain a leader. Mathematical concepts were especially difficult for Amy, and most required repeated and varied explanations. In the writing classroom, Amy's writings were brief and undeveloped. However, she approached each assignment or writing task with eagerness and a desire to do her best.

These four children welcomed me into their writing classroom. They became my teachers, showing me their struggles and successes in writing. I would sit among them with a chair drawn closely alongside their desks. My task was to listen to their insights and try to see the significance in what they considered ordinary.

I wanted to become a more astute observer of these children. I wanted to learn something about how they were learning to write. Throughout this experience, I was challenged to look for new ways of seeing and solving problems in writing. I was learning how to become an *insightful* teacher.

Reflection Point 1.2

1. Seek to understand the writers in your classroom. Pull your chair next to a writer in progress and begin to generate insight from conversations and events that seem familiar. What can you learn about young writers through careful observation? Jot down your observations in a log book.

2. Examine your writing later and think about new ways of seeing that will enable you to learn from your experience.

What Is the Classroom Setting?

The School

When approaching the large school that housed these students, I first noticed the brightly colored roof, the well-manicured park that sits adjacent to the building, and the large, sturdy wooden playset filled with laughing children. Several small bicycles haphazardly lined the bike rack.

Also noticeable was the new home construction directly across the street. From the school's front door, one could easily view the busy construction workers, the muddied vacant lots, the "For Sale" signs, and the weeds sprouting at the edges of property lines. The smell of freshly cut lumber lingered. All these elements provided evidence of rapid growth in the immediate area.

Surrounding the school was a residential area with a mix of homes. Most homes were modest, less than 20 years old, and well maintained. Streets were left muddy from construction trucks; parents with strollers accompanied school children home; and adolescents adorned with backpacks, baggy bluejeans, autumn coats, and hiking boots were walking home from the bus stop after riding the city bus from school. This neighborhood was filled with young families.

A visit to the school for the fall parent orientation found the principal at the front door greeting each person, arms outstretched. He welcomed each family individually with a handshake and a smile. Once inside the school, the chatter of children took over. Straight ahead was the library—colorful, warm, and inviting. Located in the center of the building, the library was recently home to a *Macbeth* performance by the fifth-grade class. Memories of colorful costumes, castle walls, proud parents, and excited children were captured in my thoughts. The long corridor that wound through the school led past brightly colored classrooms, a gymnasium, a music room, and an art room. Student work lined the hallway.

The Teacher

I was met each day at the classroom door by the smiling face of a colleague and friend, fifth-grade teacher Kate. We had worked together the previous spring when our common interest in children's writing united us during a graduate course on literacy education. Kate's experiences as a teacher are wide ranging. She has taught in the United States, Canada, and Kenya. I regret that Kate's real name must remain anonymous because she is an outstanding teacher dedicated to her students, and she deserves recognition. I will always be grateful for her support and guidance during my years as a graduate student. Kate played an important role in developing my understanding of young writers. She has taught me a tremendous amount about teaching and learning by allowing me to learn from the students in her classroom.

When this collaboration began, Kate was in the beginning stages of implementing a writing workshop in her classroom. This was the second year for her to investigate in her classroom the ideas of Nancie Atwell, Lucy Calkins, and Donald Graves. These three founders of writing process theory bring writing instruction alive for the teacher of young children. Atwell (1987), Calkins (1994), and Graves (1994) provide detailed descriptions and guidelines for teaching writing with a process approach. Kate wanted to explore these ideas about the writing process and provide a place where students could become comfortable with their role as writers. With the support of additional adults in her classroom (teacher's assistant and learning assistance teacher), Kate created a learning environment that engaged students in writing and encouraged them to help one another on important writing pieces.

However, the process of implementing writing workshop was bumpy. Kate experienced both success and frustration during the initial stages. Her beginning goal was to help students feel comfortable with the workshop routine. She wanted these young writers to manage their way independently through a writing process that involved creating ideas for writing, finding a theme to develop, drafting, revising, and editing. Success would come by developing a trusting community in which students felt comfortable sharing their writing with others. An obstacle for Kate was the wide range of activity within the classroom. Students were focused but working on so many different things at once. Over time, there evolved an overwhelming feeling of doubt that caused her to ask, "How does one teacher address the writing needs of so many?"

Because this was the second time Kate had welcomed me into her room, I was fully aware of her classroom procedures and expectations. Our way of working together quickly picked up where we had left off, with no specific introductions or directions necessary. Furthermore, because our previously established professional relationship continued, no time was spent initiating rapport.

The Classroom

Kate's classroom, which was spacious and bright, had 22 desks arranged in pairs. The walls were covered with colorful bulletin boards, posters, photographs, and student work. Math graphs, student-made flags, paper globes, and writing samples adorned the room. A prominently displayed poster read, "If you believe it, you can achieve it." Photographs taken during a recent *Macbeth* performance were displayed proudly on the back wall. A bulletin board with a writing theme was displayed at the front of the room. This bulletin board was a place where student writing samples were shared and regularly rotated for all to read. The bulletin board also provided a place where workshop routines and specific writing strategies could be posted.

Kate set the stage each week for a predictable and consistent writing environment. The structure of her writing period was modeled after Nancie Atwell's writing workshops (Atwell, 1987). Forty-five minutes were set aside each day for writing. During this writing time, students were free to choose their topics and work at their own pace. Student work was collected in writing portfolios. This student-centered curriculum ensured that each day in this classroom was unique. However, a consistent routine in which students were invited to explore and discover their writing process had been established.

Reflection Point 1.3 _____

1. Observe a classroom implementing a writing workshop. Take notes outlining the events of the writing period.
   - How is the classroom organized?
   - How is the class time structured?
   - What major activities are students involved in?

2. Reflect on the following questions as you analyze your notes (data).
   - What did you learn?
   - What were the students learning?
   - What was the role of the writing teacher in this environment?

- What was the role of the student writers?
- What were the positive aspects of this classroom environment?
- What questions or tensions surfaced in your mind?

The Writing Workshop

Following recess, students entered the classroom with red cheeks and tousled hair. These young writers retrieved their writing workshop binders from their storage bins and returned quietly to their desks. By the time Kate arrived, many students already had begun writing. The routine was well established. Students sifted through their binders, recalling their progress from the previous day. Each student's three-ringed binder snapped as the students removed or replaced favorite pieces of writing. Some decided to start a new piece, whereas others continued revising old drafts. Papers shuffled, pencils scratched, and students whispered; these were the sounds of students working diligently. Some students sat straight up; others slumped down in their chairs. Students twirled pencils between their fingers. These first few moments of activity provided the organizational time necessary for students to collect their thoughts and make decisions about what they would work on during the writing workshop.

Kate then began with a quick class conference in which individual students identified in a few words their task for the day. For instance, Nicole needed a teacher conference for her story titled, "Eight Easy Ways on How to Get in Trouble." Sarah was starting a new piece about Lauren's party. Daniel would continue his story about baseball, although Victoria needed to conduct a peer conference with Kenda about her story, "I'm Not a Regular Kid." Brad had just completed his final revisions and would be "publishing," Elizabeth would write her final draft of "My Summer Holiday," and Mark was not sure what he was writing about next. Kate made a note of each student's comments in her daily log. This dialogue initiated an implicit contract between student and teacher for the day's work. It also informed others about student progress, providing ideas or connections for further writing.

The remaining 35 to 40 minutes were for writing. Students drafted, revised, edited, or collaborated in peer conferences, as they chose. The three adults in the room divided their time between monitoring and conferencing. Sometimes, the adults moved around the room providing information or answering questions. Each liked to get a sense of what was being written and how students were progressing. At other times, these adults conferenced with individual students concerning works in progress.

During writing workshop, children's whispers could be heard from all corners of the room. Students were busy with their work of being authors, and they huddled together reading one another's work. These students provided support for their peers and learned from one another. This classroom invited active learning, and the children were engaged in the process of writing. (See Box 1.1 for resources about the writing process.)

Throughout the afternoon, peers gathered into groups, broke up, and formed groups again. Children working individually worked intently. Teachers walked among them, talking with one child, then another. The time seemed to go by quickly, and soon it was time to go home. Students cleaned up their desks and other working areas, putting away pencils, papers, binders, and books. They packed up their homework and put on their coats over layers of T-shirts, sweatshirts, and sweaters, then they scrambled out the door.

Further descriptions of the four individual students I studied, the classroom context, and the writing workshop routines will be shared throughout this book. Let me next position myself within the context of this experience and share my story.

Who Am I?

My interest in young writers evolved throughout my teaching career. I began teaching in Sultan, Washington, USA, where I taught third grade in a rural school district. As a beginning teacher, I worked very hard to teach reading and mathematics in an overcrowded classroom. Writing was taught with the traditional methods I had grown up experiencing. The traditional curriculum of the 1960s and 1970s placed emphasis on direct instruction, with strong teacher control and passive learners. This

---

Box 1.1
Further Reading About the Writing Process

If you are interested in exploring the writing process, you may want to seek out these foundational books:

Atwell, N. (1987). *In the middle: Writing, reading, and learning with adolescents*. Portsmouth, NH: Boynton/Cook.

Calkins, L.M. (1983). *Lessons from a child: On the teaching and learning of writing*. Portsmouth, NH: Heinemann.

Calkins, L.M. (1994). *The art of teaching writing*. Portsmouth, NH: Heinemann.

Graves, D.H. (1983). *Writing: Teachers and children at work*. Portsmouth, NH: Heinemann.

Graves, D.H. (1994). *A fresh look at writing*. Portsmouth, NH: Heinemann.

Murray, D.M. (1996). *Write to learn* (5th ed.). Fort Worth, TX: Harcourt Brace.

---

transmissional curriculum left me with few personal writing experiences to guide my teaching. My experiences writing lesson plans, report cards, grocery lists, or letters never qualified me as a *real* writer. As a result, the underlying assumption in my classroom was that children would learn to write simply by being asked to write. I needed more specific guidance to support young writers effectively.

I moved on to teach prekindergarten in a suburb of St. Louis, Missouri, USA. It was here that I experienced children's innate desire to write. These very young children wanted to write all the time. They wanted to explore a variety of writing utensils and found great pleasure in their written products. I provided regular activities for the children to write using pens, pencils, markers, crayons, chalk, and paint. During this time, my own two children were growing and entering the upper elementary grades. I could see something happening as students progressed from prekindergarten into fourth, fifth, and sixth grades: When older elementary students were confronted with the task of writing, their level of excitement for the activity had dwindled since their early school years. Why?

To answer my increasing number of questions, I began to work on my Master of Education degree at the University of Saskatchewan. I had a desire to connect with new knowledge and current research in the area of literacy education. I quickly saw that in the teaching profession we have some distance to go to give writing the place it deserves in the curriculum. Often, the teaching of writing lies somewhere behind other kinds of instruction. Recent literature on writing instruction has provided an awareness of the writing process and how children learn to write (see, for example, Atwell, 1987; Calkins, 1994; Graves, 1994). This information has brought many positive changes to the writing classroom, but it has not yet translated into practical writing methodologies for young writers who struggle with the process. For this reason, I wanted to explore further the learning patterns of the struggling writer.

Over the past several years, my professional goal has been to become personally familiar with the complex writing process. In my studies, I have completed several assignments that have intimately acquainted me with the joys and frustrations of writing. After sweating through the composing process, I admit I now have more empathy for student writers. Knowing how it feels to struggle with a piece of writing provided me with opportunities to bring insight and experience into the writing classroom. This allowed me to understand how important it is for teachers to write with their students. As we write, we can model our own writing process while making visible to students effective ways of solving writing difficulties.

My specific focus on struggling writers has also been the result of a personal story—that of my daughter, Jenna, who has been the driving influence behind my interest in this area. When Jenna was diagnosed as having a writing learning disability, I was left with many unanswered questions. As a parent, I had a fierce determination to do whatever was necessary to improve Jenna's writing ability, yet at times I felt drowned in confusion. I came to realize that no matter how determined I was or how much I wanted to help, I would not be effective until I knew what to do and how to do it. In other words, I needed the vocabulary and knowledge to make sure Jenna received the kind of help that was most effective for her particular needs.

In this profession, we often chart new directions and find our passions because of a highly personal and individual experience. I will never forget the first parent-teacher conference after my daughter had been diagnosed with a writing learning disability. The conference was filled with discussion of her many learning gaps. Focus was placed on all the things she could not do. I had never viewed *my* child that way. Until that point, I saw only her successes. I watched her growth, and I cherished the small steps she took. I found myself frustrated with a teacher who viewed her from a totally different perspective. Why did her teacher see only her disability?

What began as a personal interest became a professional obsession. Frustrating for me was the realization that my previous experiences as a teacher did not guarantee me success in understanding Jenna's difficulty. I wanted to organize, clarify, and understand as much information as possible from an educator's perspective. I wanted to look closely at the difficulties struggling writers experience, and I wanted to become comfortable with teaching and learning strategies that may help struggling writers overcome their writing difficulties.

Classroom observations and interviews for this study generated from my experiences as a parent. My background with Jenna provided me with insight into students who experience difficulty with the writing process: I have lived their frustrations amid nightly assignments and homework; I have been able to recognize the insecurities that surface when pencils are placed in their hands; I have watched teachers inadvertently overlook the strengths of these students in a system that emphasizes their weaknesses. My parent voice has become too passionate to be silenced.

Throughout this research, I have approached the experience from the perspective of teacher, researcher, and parent. As a teacher of struggling writers, I wanted to better understand how educators can best scaffold writing growth. As a researcher of struggling writers, I wanted to give a voice to these students and encourage my teaching colleagues to listen closely, appreciate, and learn from these students' stories. As a parent of a struggling writer, I wanted to view students from a growth perspective. This book contains elements from each perspective.

The roles of teacher, researcher, and parent can be symbiotic. My research and teaching experiences provided me with knowledge of the classroom and how young students learn, whereas my parenting experience provided me with the sensitivity and understanding needed to work with struggling writers. The following quote captures this relationship:

> My subjectivity is the basis for the story that I am able to tell. It is a strength on which I build. It makes me who I am as a person and as a researcher, equipping me with the perspectives and insights that shape all that I do as a researcher, from the selection of topic clear through to the emphases I make in my writing. Seen as virtuous, subjectivity is something to capitalize on rather than to exorcise. (Glesne & Peshkin, 1992, p. 104)

Why Am I Writing This Book?

During the research study that undergirds this book, I had an opportunity to study writing issues at the classroom level. I wanted to discover ways to support struggling writers and gain insight into their writing by being involved in their processes as they wrote. I wanted to look closely at the writing strategies used by young students and help them take their next steps toward growth. Above all, I wanted to recognize the growth of student participants and learn to watch for indicators of progress.

Researching young writers has helped me understand the prominent role writing should play in any elementary classroom. The teaching of writing is important to struggling students because they do far more than learn to write. While composing, students learn to make choices and carry out decisions. They learn to generate ideas, ask questions, solve problems, and develop meaning. Writing engages students as active learners and provides opportunities for developing thought. Over the past few years, I have become an advocate for making the necessary changes important for the success of struggling writers. A primary goal of this book is to bring forward the issues of young struggling writers and encourage teachers to listen closely to their stories.

As teachers, many of us have grown in our understanding of the writing process approach to teaching writing. This approach, which advocates writing through the steps of prewriting, drafting, revising, editing, and publishing, has brought many positive changes to the writing classroom (see Box 1.1 on page 11 for further reading on the writing process). However, recent research has shown that process-based writing may not be enough to help struggling writers overcome many of the difficulties they face (Graham & Harris, 1994). Reviewing recent literature reveals that struggling writers may require a more balanced approach to writing instruction (Collins, 1998; Englert, 1990; Harris & Graham, 1992; MacArthur, Schwartz, & Graham, 1991). Balancing skills and processes may be an important component in improving the writing abilities of students who struggle with the process. Therefore, a second goal of this book is to demonstrate how writing strategies *and* process writing can be integrated in the writing classroom. Within the context of student writing, greater support can be provided for students who experience difficulty. Teachers are in a position to help students think strategically about writing and provide direction that encourages them to solve the problems they encounter.

What Do I Believe About Teaching and Learning?

As a child, my first kite was red, blue, and yellow with the face of a clown looking down on me. I could not put that kite together. I wanted to, but I did not know how. It was my father who carefully tied the knots to each string. And as I watched, he demonstrated. He showed me the intricacies of kite making, all the while talking about the wind. From these first lessons, I was able to take my kite outside and watch it fly. I can put a kite together now.

Vygotsky (1934/1978) writes, "What a child can do with assistance today she will be able to do by herself tomorrow" (p. 87). Vygotsky's theory has contributed to my understanding of how children learn to write. The role of a teacher in the writing classroom can be much like that of my father's. We can provide learners the scaffolding necessary to support and extend their learning. I believe teachers play an important role in moving writing growth forward. Bruner (1986) and Applebee and Langer (1983) also support instructional scaffolding as an important teaching tool in the writing classroom. A teacher's intervention can provide a supportive tool for learners, extending their skills and allowing them to accomplish a task not otherwise possible. Spiegel (1994) notes, "It is through scaffolding that adults model mature performance of the task" (p. 83). In other words, when children are engaged in activities with more knowledgeable others, they learn from their experiences.

I also believe in the social and collaborative nature of literacy learning. Instruction requires a collaborative effort between teacher and student, so both teacher and student must come to the learning experience as partners. Collaborating with students in the learning process requires that teachers support and extend student thinking through conversation and questioning. It also requires that students take ownership for their own learning by becoming actively involved in the process. In the writing classroom, teaching becomes a joint venture in which teacher and student share the responsibility for learning.

In addition to these beliefs, I entered this experience with assumptions on which my observations were based. I believe that *all* students can grow as writers. The achievements of those who struggle are at times wide ranging and remarkable. However, most often, progress is slow and quiet. If you are not watching closely, students' accomplishments in writing can go unnoticed. Ensuring that these students felt good about themselves as writers was of critical importance to me. If these students felt successful and viewed writing as a joy, not a chore, I believed that they would make progress, no matter how small.

Reflection Point 1.4

1. Reflect and write in your journal about your beliefs about teaching and learning. Do you have a distinctive teaching style? What makes your teaching unique? What do you believe about teaching and learning? How will these beliefs and values follow you into the writing classroom? What do you value about your role as an elementary classroom teacher of writing?

2. After you have identified your own beliefs on teaching and learning, observe the teaching of two other writing instructors. Identify the qualities that make these two teachers unique. What do they know, believe, and value about the teaching of writing? What qualities do they have that you would like to emulate in your teaching? Write an analysis of your observations.

Chapter 2

Seeking to Understand
the Struggling Writer

I'm never going to get my writing up on the bulletin board. Who is going to want to read it anyway?

Kenda

Struggling writers present a unique challenge to the elementary classroom teacher. Their writing differs from more abled writers in both process and product. Along with their specific writing difficulties, struggling writers may exhibit a number of other behavioral, cognitive, or emotional problems such as poor self-concept or a low tolerance for frustration. For many of these students, feelings of inadequacy surface easily. They may experience difficulty in areas such as following directions, beginning or completing assignments, maintaining concentration, or remaining in their seats. In addition, some of these writers may also rush through their work without adequate reflection.

To understand struggling writers in the elementary classroom, it is first necessary to agree on a definition of the term. In this book, the students I present are those who experience difficulty meeting the demands of writing. Much of the research I will present is based on learning disabled children. However, I feel it is necessary to include more than this group of students in my definition. The student writers I will focus on are inefficient learners who may not apply effective learning strategies when needed. These learners possess poor strategies for approaching the complex task of writing and, therefore, are unable to meet their writing potential. My definition of a "struggling writer" purposely remains broad to include the many different types of inefficient learners who may benefit from an increased awareness of writing and the writing process. As Pressley and Levin (1986) point out, "Inefficient learners perform below normal levels but can perform at higher levels if they are led to process information differently than they usually do" (p. 175).

It is my hope that this book will provide insight into the world of young struggling writers by exploring their thoughts, emotions, and abilities. Dillon (2000) reminds us that a great deal of insight can be gained by watching, listening, and seeking to understand students as they interact in the classroom. Throughout this experience, I sought to understand the literacy needs of young writers. As I worked with Kate's students, I was looking for ways to "see more" and become awake to events as they happened. I watched facial expressions, classroom interactions, and student routines. I watched students write their pieces, read their pieces, reread their pieces, stumble onto new topics, struggle with writers' block, develop ideas, add supporting details, conference with peers, and publish final copies. During my visits in Kate's classroom, I learned how to pay attention to the children. I learned to see these students as my teachers.

Reflection Point 2.1

1. Think about a specific student in your classroom who experiences difficulty writing. Observe this student as he or she writes. What type of writing activity is this student most often involved in? What are his or her writing habits and behaviors? What could this child be thinking as he or she writes?

2. Write a short description of your observation and insights.

Initial Observations of Kenda

> *"I just want to write a real story…you know, the kind other people can read."*

When I arrived in the classroom, Kenda had not written much. It was November 4, but the only writing in her portfolio was dated September

16. Nearly 2 months had passed since she began the poem in Figure 1.

Kenda's writing struggles set her apart from the rest of the class. For her, the physical task of handwriting was unhurried and deliberate. While writing, she carefully formed each letter. When a letter was the wrong

Figure 1
Kenda's Writing Sample

size, formed incorrectly, or slanted a little too much, Kenda erased it and started over. She would erase and rewrite, erase and rewrite, erase and rewrite. Her writing evolved letter by letter. As a result, Kenda's amazing story ideas became blurred as time passed. Her initial story ideas were clear and developed when she spoke, but as her thoughts became spread out over several days, her original ideas became fuzzy. "I forget what I'm writing about each day," she would tell me. She struggled to maintain a sense of the whole composition.

Kenda was also easily distracted, pausing after writing each letter to think and gaze around the room. When I sat next to Kenda, I could direct and redirect her attention toward her writing, which helped. However, the minute I stepped away, Kenda's writing slowed down again.

Despite Kenda's daily struggles to remain focused on her writing, she was a pleasant and cheerful child. Her conversations were inviting, her ideas for her pieces were amazing, and she spoke fluently about her work. Kenda's struggles with writing were serious, yet she articulated her thoughts well:

> Just like sometimes I can make up really good stories and sometimes I can make up really good brainstorms and sometimes I can't come up with good things. Writing isn't really that easy. I don't know what I could say that is really easy about writing. Maybe when someone has help from another person, then writing gets easier and easier. You get to figure out the story and figure out what it is you are doing…. I have the hardest time with spelling. I can't spell the words I write down…like in this word *apple*. I spelled it a-p-p-e-l. That is what I have problems with. But the teacher gives us help. She asks us what is our idea. She helps us read over it and then she, like says, "Maybe you can try and think a little bit more. If you think of the story in your head and picture it like you are just there watching the whole thing, even though you might not be there…if you could picture it in your head, you could write it down on paper."

I marveled at how well Kenda could talk about a process that was difficult for her. Her oral language and verbal skills were good. She just had difficulty assigning written words to her thoughts and conversations. What happened between her head and her hands? She articulated her thoughts clearly with language, but found it difficult to communicate her ideas through writing.

One reason Kenda may have been experiencing writing difficulty "may be attributed to the complexity of the cognitive processes involved" (Englert & Raphael, 1989, p. 108). Writers experience difficulty because writing is an intellectually demanding process. The complex task of writing requires the coordination of a variety of cognitive activities and requires the synthesis of many skills and abilities. Kenda was trying to generate ideas, organize her thinking, communicate something the reader did not understand, sequence her ideas, spell correctly, and deal with the physical aspects of handwriting—*all at the same time.* As I began to get to know Kenda as a writer, I wondered how the multiple challenges of writing might be simplified for her. How could I help make this complicated task become more manageable?

Other questions surfaced in response to Kenda's writing experiences. One day, I watched as Kenda tried to maintain a sense of confidence despite her many difficulties, as she and Victoria worked together to edit one of Kenda's recently written pieces. As I approached the girls, my excitement arose because I realized Kenda must have completed her piece and had initiated a peer edit herself. This was wonderful, and I wanted to celebrate her accomplishment! I now understood the amount of time that went into her writing and was pleased to see the pride that surfaced as a result of this progress.

As I settled in next to the girls, my excitement quickly vanished. Victoria was reading, correcting spelling; reading, correcting spelling; reading, crossing out. Kenda's story—the one she had worked so hard on—was now a crossed-out mess. Every inch of her paper was filled with red marks (see Figure 2). Most words were misspelled, and Victoria was correcting each one because that was her responsibility as a peer editor.

Whatever excitement Kenda had about her accomplishment was now gone. Any momentary pride she once felt had dissolved amidst crossed-out words and a paper that was totally marked up. Kenda lost interest in this peer conference. She began writing on the chalkboard, talking to a friend, fidgeting, and doing anything but looking at her paper. Victoria signed her name, dated the paper, and wrote, "Great story!" She handed the piece back to Kenda and returned to her own desk and her own writing. There was a moment of silence. Kenda then looked at me with her

Figure 2
Kenda's Peer-Edited Story

Hi my name is Kenda. I am not a
average kid. Well I ~~was~~ was ~~blatat~~ until
~~One~~ one day I. Was ~~wockin~~ walking home
From School. I ~~was minding~~ was minding my
~~One~~ own ~~bisins~~ bissniss as ~~usawll~~ usaual. ~~out uv~~ out of the
~~boom~~ bloom a ~~grat~~ great big green van came
by me ~~all the~~ all of a sudin I ~~hrae~~ hurd
~~sumewon~~ some one ~~yall~~ yell ~~out~~ out Look ~~out~~ out kid.
And ~~than~~ then I ~~falt~~ felt ~~simthin~~ something ~~wirde~~ wierd
on me. I Look down at my
~~arne~~ arm and I ~~nowtis~~ notissed ~~thir~~ their ~~wis~~ was
~~simthin wird~~ something weird and slimy on me.
I ~~flt~~ felt ~~fille~~ really ~~wirtid~~ weird and I ~~flt~~ felt
~~some than~~ something was ~~wird~~ weird and
~~tigaley~~ tingaley on my arm all the
Sudun. The green van was Back
~~ingojsin~~ ~~atete~~ Mc I ran in the ~~Bake~~ 2Bko
~~alle~~

(continued)

Figure 2 (continued)
Kenda's Peer-Edited Story

I hid behind a ~~grbig~~ garbage can. The man
~~how~~ who ~~was~~ was ~~drivin~~ driving The Van, did't notis me
behind The ~~grbig~~ garbage can. ~~aftr~~ after The Van ~~went~~ went by
Me I ~~waited~~ waited ~~afay minits~~ a few minutes and than I ran
home. I told ~~no won~~ noone a ~~bot~~ bought ~~anit~~ anythin
~~tine~~ that day. And if I told my mom
She ~~wood~~ would have a ~~hart a tack~~ heartattack and
if I told my dad He ~~wode~~ would go
~~Bonkfse~~ Bonkers

Wednesday November 4
great story!

large brown eyes and said solemnly, "Ms. Christenson, I just want to write
a *real* story. You know...the kind other people can read."

It was at that moment that I began to experience the tensions other
teachers must feel as they watch students expose their writing to peers.
Writing process theory (Atwell, 1987; Calkins, 1994; Graves, 1994)

supports the notion that peers can contribute significantly to writing development, yet for the struggling writer, there are problematic aspects of peer conferences. Kenda had worked hard on this piece. She had begun to gain some sense of satisfaction from her writing, and then her hard work was called into question. The peer conference opened up this sensitive writer for criticism.

As teachers, how do we make these issues explicit to a classroom filled with peers? How do we negotiate solutions when we deal with such sensitive issues? What kinds of intervention should teachers provide? These questions also framed my thinking as I interacted with Kenda and this classroom of writers.

Initial Observations of Paulo

"I don't have anything to write about."

Paulo was never very sure he wanted me around. He was resistant to conversation with me and unwilling to carry on a dialogue about his writing. My first attempts at conversation were greeted with shoulder shrugs. "Writing is boring," he would say. One day Paulo entered class after recess in a flurry. He stomped in, head down, face stern, eyes glaring, and mouth tight-lipped. "What's up, Paulo?" I asked. "I'm terrible. Just terrible," he replied. My attempts to get to the bottom of his emotions came with no luck. Paulo would not speak.

During my initial interactions with Paulo, I found myself asking questions that many teachers must ask as they are faced with distant students. How do I connect with Paulo? What can I do to find out what matters to him? How can I build on his interests and bring energy to his writing? What kinds of classroom experiences have led Paulo to become disengaged as a writer?

When Paulo decided to begin writing, topic selection was difficult for him. He struggled to settle in on a topic of interest. "I don't have anything to write about," he would say. When he finally identified a topic, his piece reflected disinterest. Little time or effort was put into his writing. He wanted it done and over. Paulo was writing to complete an assignment. Figure 3 shows a sample of Paulo's writing.

Figure 3
Paulo's Writing Sample

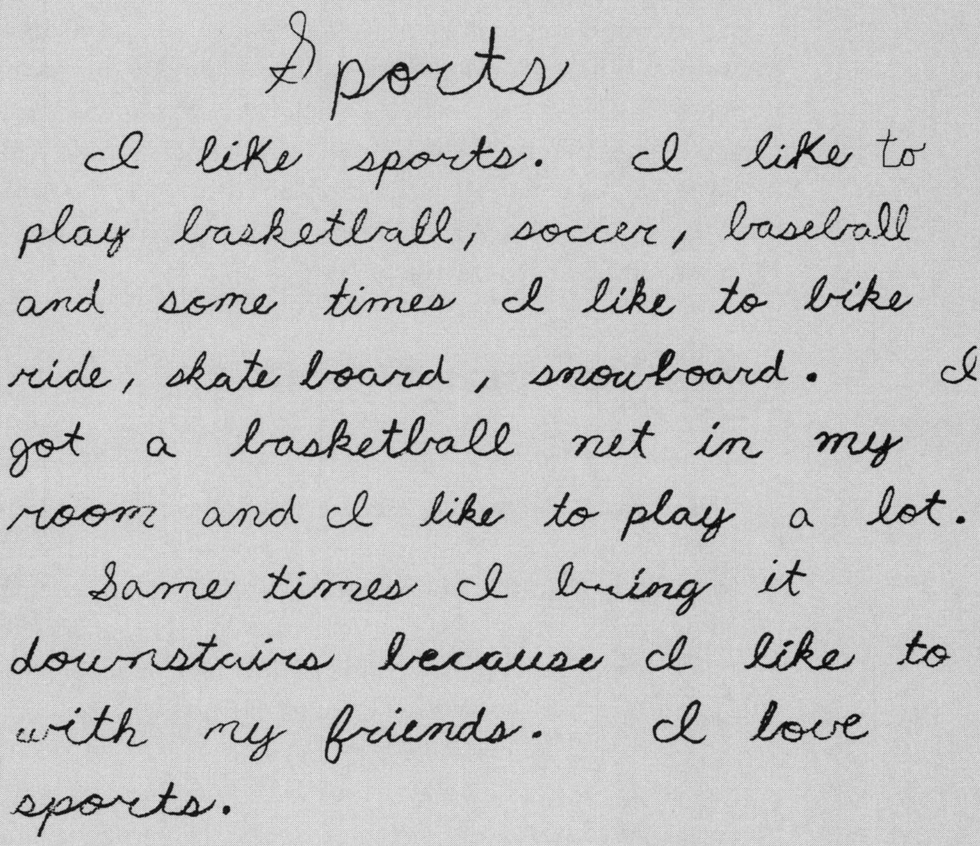

Sports

I like sports. I like to play basketball, soccer, baseball and some times I like to bike ride, skate board, snowboard. I got a basketball net in my room and I like to play a lot. Same times I bring it downstairs because I like to with my friends. I love sports.

When Paulo was in the mood, he could write fluently. He did not labor over the physical aspects of writing, and as a result, words emerged on paper quickly when we wrote. As time passed, Paulo became more motivated during the composing process but distracted and uninterested in revising or rewriting. He would say things like, "I don't want to peer edit this. I don't have to. No, I don't. I don't want to make it into a story. I'll just have to write it all over again."

There were days when Paulo was resistant to support or guidance. I just could not seem to break through his tough exterior. He showed no energy, no spark, no enthusiasm. I was not sure I was getting anywhere with him, but I kept trying. He did his best work alone, so each day I would check in with him quickly and move onto another writer.

There were brief moments when I could see a softer side to Paulo's personality. When he presented me with a holiday gift, his body language turned soft, and his voice became quiet. There was a hidden smile there somewhere. When he spoke to friends about playground happenings, his voice was passionate. Would I ever reach through to this side of him in the writing classroom? Would I ever be able to carry on a two-way conversation with him about writing?

Initial Observations of Daniel

"Spelling...just that."

Daniel was a hard worker. He quickly got to work after recess, would work right through the "Status of the Class" discussion, and would remain working throughout the writing period. No reminders were needed, no prodding, no encouragement—Daniel just wrote. I experienced how easy it could be to overlook the quiet, focused writer. Daniel demanded very little of my time but always responded eagerly to my presence.

At a glance, Daniel's daily activities and revised writing displayed writing competence; however, a look at the rough drafts of his written products told another story. Daniel struggled daily with spelling, and he wanted to learn to spell. When I initially asked him what he would like to learn next in order to become a better writer, Daniel responded, "Spelling...just that." (See Figure 4.)

Kate, Daniel's previous teachers, and Daniel's parents all had shown concern about Daniel's spelling development. Despite all the good intentions, Daniel was still experiencing spelling difficulty. Why are some students naturally good spellers, whereas others have to work hard at it? I wondered how I could best help Daniel with his spelling difficulties within the context of his writing? How would I maintain a focus on writing content, yet move Daniel's spelling growth forward? These questions framed my work with this quiet, focused writer.

**Figure 4
Daniel's Writing Sample**

My Pet Rabbet
This is my pet rabbit. His
name is Askum. His black whith white spots
and brown spats. He likes playing outside. He
likes to be petted around the eares Askum is
teree years old. He likes jumpingiton
me. He eate mys mor's plamts and
flowers. If any cat comes after my
Rabbit they will never cath him.

THE
End

Initial Observations of Amy

"Ms. Christenson—Look what I have done!"

Amy was pleasant, fun, and energetic. Each day she would happily
greet me, dash to get her writing folder, and eagerly share her work.
"Come see what I am writing!" she would request. Amy was an interesting conversationalist, and each day she shared new stories of her family

and their experiences. Throughout the class writing period, Amy frequently required my attention. She would jump up regularly and come to me with questions about her piece. Sometimes, she just wanted to share her progress. "Ms. Christenson—Look what I've done!" Amy would check in with me before she added new ideas or changed her thoughts.

Amy did have difficulty developing her ideas. Her initial pieces were predictable, brief, and filled with generalities. They were most often written

Figure 5
Amy's Writing Sample

what I did yesterday

Wednesday September . 30

Yesterday when I was doing my homework somebody rang the door bell it was my friend abby and her cousan carter he is 1½ years old. he likes to dance, *when Abby say's to dance he dance's and after a while we played Sega it was fun. 'And then she had to do her homework,*Oh yeh I finished my homework.

about her daily experiences in a diary form. Her writing included little explanation or detail. (See Figure 5.)

The lengthy conversations Amy and I shared also were filled with generalities. The language did not seem readily available to describe her thoughts or the images in her mind.

Amy:	My dad fixes lots of stuff.
Ms. C.:	What do you mean by "stuff"?
Amy:	You know, he fixes all different stuff.
Ms. C.:	Like what? Can you think of some examples?
Amy:	I don't know...all kinds of stuff.
Ms. C.:	Does he fix things around the house?
Amy:	Yeah. Things around the house. My mom likes helping Dad with all kinds of stuff. You know, like gardening and stuff...like stuff around the yard.

My questions to Amy were often met with long pauses and eye-rolling. She would think and then respond with a shoulder shrug or "I don't know."

Amy began the task of writing with little advance planning. She would organize her writing utensils on her desk and then simply begin writing. She wrote whatever came to mind at the moment. After writing a few brief thoughts, Amy would abruptly end her piece. Amy's difficulty developing her ideas and expressing thoughts in words did not inhibit her excitement for writing. She was often the first student to greet me after recess. Amy was eager to begin writing and thrived on the personal attention I could give. She welcomed our interactions and was pleased to share her writing with me.

Amy already had developed an effective spelling strategy in her writing; she would write the word the best way she knew and then circle it if it "didn't look right." She could easily identify misspelled words in her writing and often found ways to correct them herself. I looked forward to focusing on helping Amy to generate ideas, plan, and develop her thoughts.

Characteristics of Struggling Writers

What makes these students who struggled with writing in Kate's class different from other writers? We can gain a great deal of insight about these students by examining research, which has shown that the writing of struggling writers differs from more abled writers in *both* process and product (see Newcomer & Barenbaum, 1991). In the following sentences, I will identify some of the characteristics of struggling writers found in the research. Please recognize that research can position students in a way that does not reflect a growth perspective. Previous studies have assembled a profile of the young struggling writer from a deficit perspective. Rather than identifying the strengths and abilities of these young students, research has identified all the things struggling writers *cannot* do. I encourage you to look beyond the classification systems as presented. Become familiar with the abilities of young struggling writers and look for the strengths in your own students. These classification systems are presented only as a way for you to better understand the abilities of the struggling writer.

Also, please keep in mind, not all struggling writers will possess all the outlined characteristics. Students with writing problems are diverse in terms of their specific difficulties (Berninger, Abbott, Whitaker, Sylvester, & Nolen, 1995). Our challenge as educators is to identify each writer's unique combination of specific writing and processing challenges. Students' experiences cannot be characterized or generalized to others. Calkins (1983) reminds us that "although writing development is talked about 'in general,' it always happens 'in particular.' In the end, we always teach unique children..." (p. 7).

Difference in Written Products

Research has shown that the written products of struggling writers differ considerably from the written products of more abled writers. Most noticeable is the observation that struggling writers often produce products that are shorter (Barenbaum, Newcomer, & Nodine, 1987) and fewer in number (Nodine, Barenbaum, & Newcomer, 1985). Struggling writers compose very little considering the time allotted for the task.

Consider the writing sample in Figure 6, paying close attention to the dates in the written piece. The sample illustrates how much writing was completed during each of three 45-minute writing workshop periods. It is evident that this writer had difficulty producing content during the allotted time. This observation is only the first step in guiding a struggling writer toward new learning. With this initial observation, teachers can begin to ask questions such as, Why is this student less fluent than other writers? What might be interfering with production? What will help this student to generate written text? These questions can frame our work as

Figure 6
Writing Samples From Three 45-Minute Writing Workshops

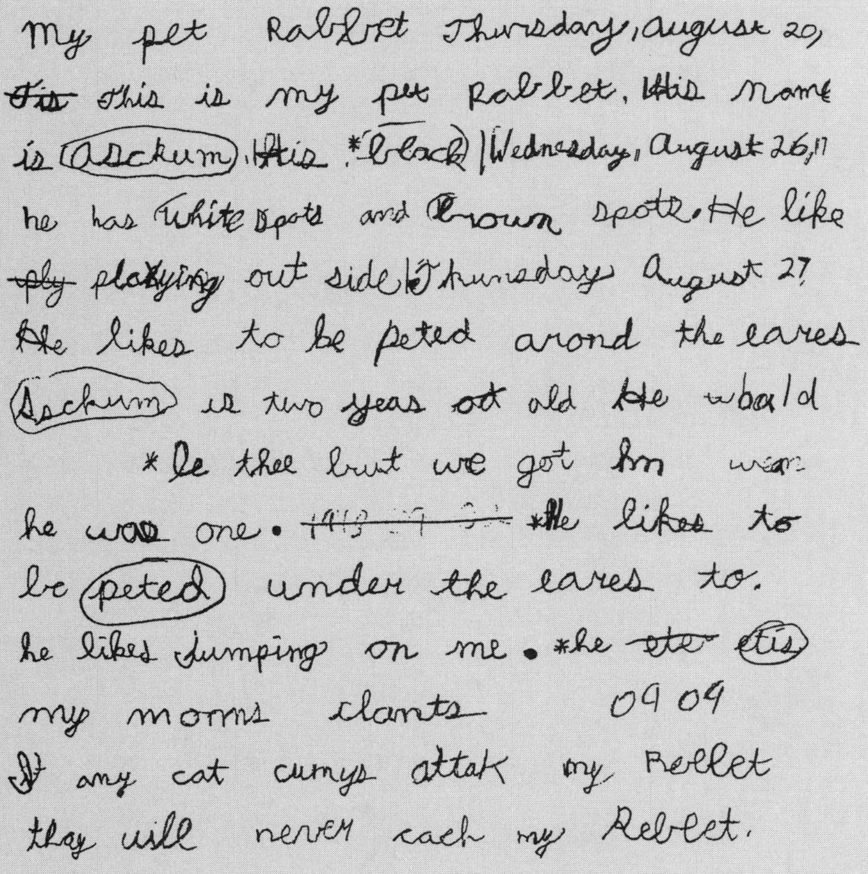

we interact with young writers who experience difficulty with writing fluency.

Research has also demonstrated that struggling writers may lack an awareness of how to organize their writing. These writers often produce less coherent papers than more-skilled writers (Montague, Maddux, & Dereshiwsky, 1990; Vallecorsa & Garriss, 1990), and experience difficulty structuring their written pieces (Englert, Raphael, Anderson, Gregg, & Anthony, 1989; Englert, Raphael, Fear, & Anderson, 1988; Thomas, Englert, & Gregg, 1987). The writing sample in Figure 7 was written by a struggling writer early in the school year.

Figure 7
Example of an Unorganized Writing Sample

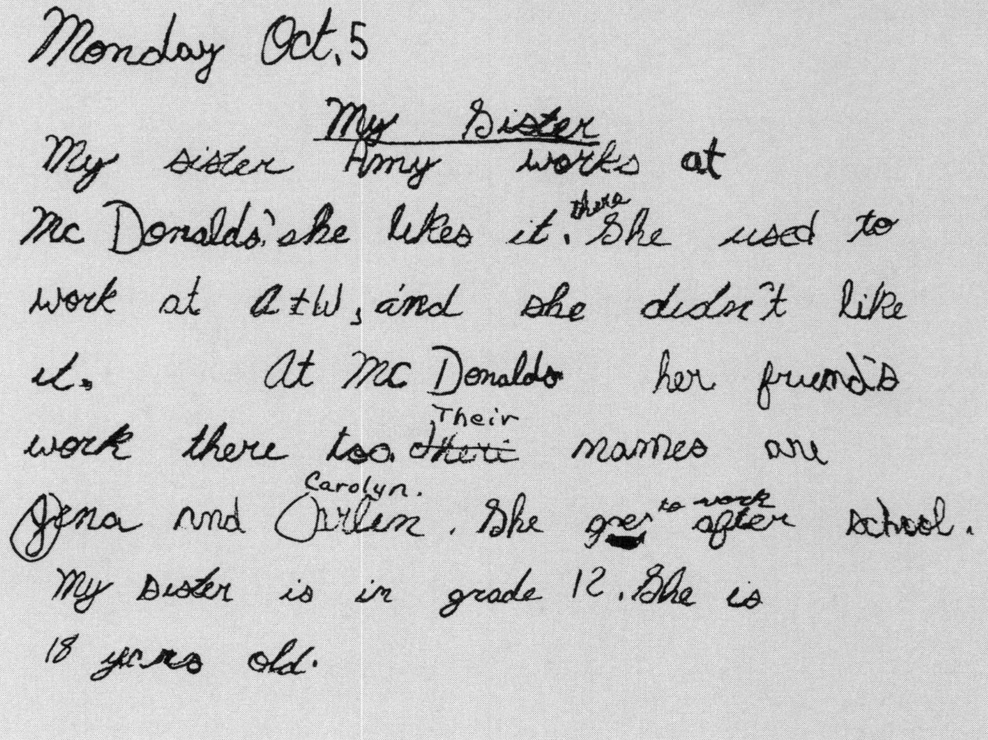
Monday Oct. 5
My Sister
My sister Amy works at
Mc Donalds' she likes it. there She used to
work at A&W, and she didn't like
it. At Mc Donalds her friend's
work there too. Their ~~there~~ names are
Jena and Carolyn. Arlen. She goes to work after school.
My sister is in grade 12. She is
18 years old.

When reviewing written products, such as the one in Figure 7, teachers observe learners writing with few ideas, incomplete or choppy sentences, and incomplete transitions. These writers leave out critical information and are not sure when or how to add detail to their pieces. The example in Figure 7 illustrates how instruction with young writers can begin with the development of their ideas and strategies for organizing their written thoughts. The student writing in Figure 7 is representative of the work of many other young writers who may also require an understanding of the detail and organization required for effective writing.

Other researchers have illustrated how struggling writers often use fewer fresh words in their writing (Morris & Crump, 1982). The variety of word choice in their written language is deficient when compared to the writing of their more skilled peers. In other words, more skilled writers will include unique and challenging words in their pieces, whereas struggling writers often include words in their writing that can be found on high-frequency word lists. (High-frequency words are those words that occur regularly in student reading and writing. For more information on high-frequency word lists, see Cunningham, 2000, pages 54–86.)

In addition to these characteristics, research has shown how handwriting and mechanics (such as spelling, capitalization, and punctuation) can also be difficult for the struggling writer. For example, the written products of those who experience difficulty writing can be difficult to read because they are filled with spelling, punctuation, and grammatical errors (Moran, 1981). The reader must work diligently to understand the meaning of the writer's message. Struggling with the mechanical aspects of writing creates problems for young writers, which often interrupts their ability to plan their thoughts. This interferes with both the quantity and quality of their work (Graham, 1990) because these obstacles can make writing a difficult and tedious task. The following writing sample illustrates a young writer's struggle with mechanics:

> it was in the sumer I was with my frind garey it was raning and I was comeing home garey was giveing me a dubel on the cete and we can a rand the cner we can clocer and clocer to my hose and We cam be sae my nabrs car and a blue car came out of no war He hets us my moms frande ran to yos the phone at her hous

In process-approach classrooms, teachers emphasize process more than product. However, it is difficult to avoid focusing on errors in the written product on the previous page. Helping this student will require talking to him about the specific spelling skills he needs to learn. The many surface and mechanical problems suggest that "content" feedback will not be enough to reconstruct this into a successful piece. It will become important for this student to develop enough fluency so that his spelling, capitalization, and punctuation problems will not interfere with the process of getting his thoughts on paper.

Difference in the Writing Process

The writing process of struggling writers also differs from the writing process of more skilled peers. Evidence suggests that struggling writers lack procedural knowledge about the writing process (Graham, Schwartz, & MacArthur, 1993). These writers are often not aware of their own writing process or their thoughts behind the task of writing. As Paulo stated, "I don't know what I do. I just do it."

If struggling writers are made aware of their writing process, they may have difficulty communicating their ideas. In Kate's classroom, my questions were often met with shoulder shrugs or one-word answers. At one point, I watched what looked like a dance while one student attempted to respond to my question through body language because the words were not coming out to express her thoughts. Struggling writers are often not well equipped to communicate or clearly articulate their thoughts. Consider the following discussion:

Ms. C.:	Do you like writing, Amy?
Amy:	Uh-huh. Yep. Uh-huh.
Ms. C.:	Why do you like it?
Amy:	I don't know. Just because.
Ms. C.:	How did you learn to write, Amy?
Amy:	I forget. It was so long ago.
Ms. C.:	Do you consider yourself to be a good writer?
Amy:	Yeah.

| Ms. C.: | Why do you think so? What makes you a good writer? |
| Amy: | Hard question. I don't know. |

Interacting with these students through conversation allowed me an opportunity to refine my questioning skills and learn to probe for further clarification. However, it became apparent that the thoughts and perceptions of struggling writers would not necessarily come forward through dialogue or discussion. These students were just learning to articulate their thoughts and feelings. They were just beginning to understand how to reply to questions in an organized and clear way, so daily conversation provided only a small glimpse into their thoughts.

Research in student writing has also demonstrated that many struggling writers may have difficulty selecting topics and generating ideas (Morrocco & Newman, 1986). This became evident as I worked with these four learners. I regularly received requests for help during the beginning stages of writing, such as

"I'm stuck...I don't know what to write about. Will you help me?"

"There is nothing to write about."

These students even recognized that the beginning stages of the writing process were difficult:

| Ms. C.: | What is the hardest part about writing, Paulo? |
| Paulo: | Thinking of ideas and trying to think of a title. Coming up with ideas is the hardest part. Oh boy. |

Once a topic or theme for their writing had been selected, these students often approached the task of writing by simply retrieving from memory whatever seemed appropriate and then writing down their immediate thoughts (MacArthur & Graham, 1987). I observed struggling writers pick up their pencils and quickly begin writing with little reflection or planning. Without any overall plan for their writing, these young writers tended to write from one sentence to the next without thinking of the entire composition as a whole. Bereiter and Scardamalia (1987) refer to this as knowledge telling: Once the topic is identified, the writer retrieves whatever information is readily available and moves forward in his or her writing.

Struggling writers are just beginning to understand the complex task of writing. These writers are not incapable writers; they are just beginning writers who need some extra help. (See Box 2.1 for further reading on characteristics of struggling writers.) As we reflect on the writing abilities of our students, it is important to reflect simultaneously on our teaching practices. As we gain insight into our students as writers, our teaching can be transformed. We can meet the growing developmental needs of our students in an effort to move writing growth forward.

Box 2.1
Additional Reading on the Struggling Writer

Avery, C.S. (1987). Traci: A learning-disabled child in a writing-process classroom. In G.D. Bissex & R.H. Bullock (Eds.), *Seeing for ourselves: Case-study research by teachers of writing* (pp. 59–75). Portsmouth, NH: Heinemann.

Cleary, L.M. (1991). *From the other side of the desk: Students speak out about writing.* Portsmouth, NH: Boynton/Cook.

Graham, S. (1992). Helping students with LD progress as writers. *Intervention in School and Clinic,* 27(3), 134–144.

Graves, D.H. (1991). All children can write. In S. Stires (Ed.), *With promise: Redefining reading and writing for "special" students* (pp. 115–126). Portsmouth, NH: Heinemann.

Rhodes, L.K., & Dudley-Marling, C. (1988). *Readers and writers with a difference: A holistic approach to teaching learning disabled and remedial students.* Portsmouth, NH: Heinemann.

Building Writing Confidence

From these initial conversations, the students and I began our work together. Each student had a fragile sense of who he or she was as a writer and regular feelings of inadequacy surfaced. I recognized their feelings in their facial expressions, body language, comments, and need for constant affirmation. I found their writing confidence to be closely tied to their writing struggles. Shaughnessy (1977) argues that struggling students "write the way they do, not because they are slow or nonverbal, indifferent to or incapable of academic excellence, but because they are beginners and must, like all beginners, learn by making mistakes" (p. 5).

Bartholomae (1980) encourages teachers to begin "instruction with what a writer *does* rather than what he fails to do" (p. 258). In a writing classroom, young writers can be viewed in terms of growth, rather than disability or deficiency (Keefe, 1996), but often we as educators look for disability rather than ability (Roller, 1996). In many classrooms, the growth of struggling writers has been measured against the progress of other children. Even as these struggling writers gain knowledge, they continue to remain behind their peers in writing achievement. Their gains often come slowly and can be discounted easily when compared to the progress of others. How easy it can be to focus on areas of weakness, often leaving growth unrecognized. But, as Rose (1989) states,

> If you set up the right conditions, try as best you can to cross class and cultural boundaries, figure out what's needed to encourage performance...if you watch and listen, again and again there will emerge evidence of ability that escapes those who dwell on differences. (p. 222)

When I think reflectively about students who struggle with the writing process, I marvel at how far they can come despite their learning challenges. As Graves (1983, 1985, 1991, 1994) repeatedly reminds us, all students can grow as writers. These students may struggle with writing, yet they experience success. Recognizing growth becomes a critical part of moving these students toward effective writing. With this insight, I began each writing conference looking for the things the four students *could* do as writers. These students were very aware of their specific difficulties, but they were not as aware of their strengths. In our initial conversations, their comments focused on their difficulties. Although they all had acquired many writing skills and strategies throughout their years as students, they tended to focus on the things they *could not* do.

Ms. C.:	Do you consider yourself to be a good writer?
Kenda:	[shakes her head "no"]
Ms. C.:	Why not?
Kenda:	I can't think of good stories very much. I can't really spell. I can't spell at all.
Ms. C.:	Have you ever written something you are really proud of?
Kenda:	No.

Ms. C.:	Do you consider yourself to be a good writer?
Paulo:	I don't think I'm that good or anything…
Ms. C.:	What do you do really well when you write? What are you good at?
Paulo:	Hmmm…That's a tough question.
Ms. C.:	Do you consider yourself to be a good writer, Daniel?
Daniel:	Ah…I don't know. I guess so.
Ms. C.:	What makes you a good writer, Amy?
Amy:	Hard question.
Ms. C.:	What are you really good at when you write?
Amy:	I don't know. I can't think of one thing.
Ms. C.:	I can think of one thing.
Amy:	What?
Ms. C.:	You choose the best topics. I can tell you write about things that are important to you. I can tell that the topics you choose are topics you want to write about. Is that right?
Amy:	Uh-huh.
Ms. C.:	Have you ever written something…that you have been really proud of?
Amy:	No.
Ms. C.:	You've never written anything really good?
Amy:	Oh, no!

Somewhere down the road, these students had lost positive perceptions of themselves as writers. Missing was a sense of knowing when they did something really well. Each day they needed positive reminders of their achievements and encouragement to work. These reminders were often met with the students' puzzled looks or doubtful eyes, because they always questioned their abilities.

As time passed, the classroom teacher and I worked to identify their writing strengths and weaknesses. We tried to help them think critically, build on their writing strengths, and problem solve around their writing weaknesses. Throughout this experience, I clearly did not want to play the role of "writing teacher expert." These four students and I worked together, placing *their* thoughts at the forefront of our discussions as much as possible. I wanted the students to begin to believe in their own choices and decisions, and to rely on their own judgment. Above all, I wanted these students to gain confidence in their writing abilities.

Reflection Point 2.2

1. Initiate conversations with your students that will bring forward their thoughts and attitudes on writing. Take notes on your conversations. Ask questions such as, Do you like writing? Why or why not? Do you consider yourself to be a good writer? How do you know? Have you ever written something you have been especially proud of? What difficulties or problems do you have as a writer? What would you like to learn next in order to become a better writer?

2. Read over students' responses and reflect on what you learned about individual students from these interactions.

The Writing Process Approach

Historically, when students experienced difficulty with writing, their remedial instruction separated them from the classroom environment and into individual or small-group instruction where they started over, repeating the skills and drills they had already failed. This traditional approach advocated skills, strategies, and rules for writing that were imposed on students by the teacher who served as the expert. Students were encouraged to master small parts and subskills before attempting whole pieces of writing.

The field of writing has seen a shift away from traditional writing instruction, however, toward a process approach (Hairston, 1982), which encourages students to experience the writing processes of prewriting, drafting, revising, editing, and publishing (Graves, 1983; Murray, 1996; see also Box 2.2). Research has greatly influenced our understanding writing as a process to be experienced, rather than only a product to be evaluated. This approach emphasizes the communicative purpose of writing by establishing communities for writing within the classroom. Students write for meaningful purposes and real audiences. Students are active participants in a learning process in which writing is viewed as a social and collaborative experience.

In many classrooms the process approach is implemented as a writing workshop (Atwell, 1987; Calkins, 1994). Here, environments are created that provide the time needed for student writing. Students write individual pieces daily and receive regular responses to their writing from peers and teachers. Within this environment, students are encouraged to write for themselves as a tool for reflection and personal learning.

Teaching writing as a process has brought many positive changes to writing classrooms. As I observed the four student participants growing as writers within a writing workshop, I could visibly see how process-oriented writing instruction was especially beneficial to struggling writers. First, a workshop environment provides daily opportunities for students to write. Children cannot be expected to generate ideas and complete written products during one brief writing period per week. Kenda, Paulo, Daniel, and Amy required daily time to begin to understand this complex task. By implementing writing workshops, teachers encourage students to work on the same piece of writing across many writing sessions. The regular, sustained writing provided within this environment helped these four writers learn to make choices and carry out decisions. It provided the time they needed to learn to identify and solve writing dilemmas, which was key to moving their writing growth forward.

Graves (1985) emphasizes that topic choice is at the heart of successful writing and is key to writing growth. Kate encouraged these four writers to choose their own topics for writing, and this choice became a powerful motivator. Helping these four young students tap into their own interests became an effective starting point for engaging them in learning.

Box 2.2
The Five Stages of the Writing Process

Stage 1—Prewriting

This involves everything the writer does before beginning the actual task of writing, including activating background knowledge, generating ideas, and making plans for approaching the writing task.

Stage 2—Drafting

Drafting is the process of getting ideas down on paper. When this stage is completed, the writer has finished his or her first draft.

Stage 3—Revising

Revisions require that writers take a second look at their piece. Good writing often reflects good rewriting of a piece.

Stage 4—Editing

Once the content and organization of a piece are set, the writer can edit and proofread the piece for spelling, punctuation, capitalization, and word choice.

Stage 5—Publishing

Publishing invites students to share their writing with others and celebrate their work. This can involve read-aloud sessions, display of finished pieces, the creation of a book, or class-produced newspapers, books, and magazines.

Kenda, Paulo, Daniel, and Amy wrote most comfortably about the topics with which they were familiar because information on their chosen topic was readily available, and because they felt personally connected to their work. When these students were writing about matters of personal importance, they found the energy and motivation to continue. In addition, I was fascinated to see that for these students who struggled, encouraging self-selected topics made fewer demands on their organizational and planning skills.

Workshop settings are especially beneficial to the struggling writer because they accommodate individual difference. In process-approach classrooms, where student ability varies, opportunities can be provided for all writers to work at their own pace and on their own level. Tasks can be selected that are meaningful and appropriate to individual writers. Workshop classrooms accommodate individual differences and contribute significantly to the many ability levels in any given classroom, which is especially significant for the writer who faces challenges with the process.

Within this environment, struggling writers can spend time working on relevant tasks. They need not spend time on writing exercises that are not appropriate to their instructional needs. Also, activities and routines within the workshop classroom apply to *all* children, so struggling writers are allowed to function as full and equal members of the writing community (Avery, 1987). Further, because students are not differentiated according to ability, workshop classrooms can accommodate a wide range of students and a wide range of abilities.

The activities promoted by writing workshop (Atwell, 1987) have undoubtedly been beneficial for all student writers, even those who struggle. However, recent writing research has shown that process-based writing may not be enough to help struggling writers overcome many of their difficulties (Graham & Harris, 1994). These students often require more intensive instruction and greater support, which can be provided by combining instruction in process writing with writing strategies. Embedding strategy instruction within the process approach can help achieve a balance in the development of skills and processes. This balanced approach encourages students to think strategically and learn how to solve problems they encounter when writing. (For more information on integrating strategy instruction and process writing in the elementary writing classroom, see Box 2.3 and Chapter 4.)

Box 2.3
Additional Reading on Integrating Strategy Instruction and Writing Process

Collins, J.L. (1998). *Strategies for struggling writers*. New York: Guilford.

Danoff, B., Harris, K.R., & Graham, S. (1993). Incorporating strategy instruction within the writing process in the regular classroom: Effects on the students with and without learning disabilities. *Journal of Reading Behavior, 25*(3), 295–322.

Englert, C.S. (1990). Writing through strategy instruction. In T.E. Scruggs & B.Y.L. Wong (Eds.), *Intervention research in learning disabilities* (pp. 186–223). New York: Springer-Verlag.

Harris, K.R., & Graham, S. (1992). *Helping young writers master the craft: Strategy instruction and self-regulation in the writing process*. Cambridge, MA: Brookline.

Harris, K.R., & Graham, S. (1996). Memo to constructivists: Skills count, too. *Educational Leadership, 53*, 26–29.

MacArthur, C.A., Schwartz, S.S., Graham, S., Molloy, D., & Harris, K. (1996). Integration of strategy instruction into a whole language classroom: A case study. *Learning Disabilities Research and Practice, 11*(3), 168–176.

Reflection Point 2.3_____

1. How do you view the teaching of writing?

2. How is writing taught in your classroom?

3. What aspects of process-oriented instruction do you see as beneficial?

4. How might you consider balancing writing skills, strategies, and process within a workshop environment?

_____

Chapter 3

Supporting Students
as They Grow as Writers

Ms. C.:	*What do you do when you get stuck while writing?*
Kenda:	*I stop and think...then I ask the teacher.*
Paulo:	*I sit down and think and think and think... until my head hurts.*
Daniel:	*I just go on and then I ask my friend.*
Amy:	*I don't know.*

Struggling writers often do not know what to do when they encounter a problem in writing. Many seem to be missing the ability to problem solve their *own* way out of a writing difficulty. When Kenda, Paulo, Daniel, and Amy encountered a writing difficulty, their only solution was to leave the responsibility for problem solving to an outside source, either a friend or a teacher. Struggling writers often do not know what to do when they are faced with a writing predicament, and frustration mounts with no visible way of identifying or solving their own problems.

Metacognitive Knowledge and the Struggling Writer

Englert and colleagues (1988) suggest that the difficulties experienced by struggling writers may be traced to a lack of metacognitive knowledge. These writers lack important knowledge about when, why, and how to use writing strategies (Pressley & Levin, 1986). Researchers (Collins,

1998; Gagne, 1985) have defined three types of metacognitive knowledge: declarative knowledge, procedural knowledge, and conditional knowledge. Declarative knowledge provides the content for writing. It includes knowledge stored in our memory about a topic, as well an awareness of how to go about obtaining additional content knowledge. Declarative knowledge addresses the question, *What* is my writing goal? Procedural knowledge provides the strategies for planning, writing, and revising. Procedural knowledge asks, *How* shall I accomplish my writing goal? Conditional knowledge supplies information concerning *when* and *why* to apply specific strategies such as, *When* shall I use a specific strategy, and *why* is it important for me to use this strategy?

The three types of metacognitive knowledge can be further distinguished in terms of Paulo's writing. Early in the school year, Paulo wrote a story about his favorite sport, basketball. Declarative knowledge provided Paulo with the information he needed to write about the sport: What is basketball? How might he describe the sport to an outsider? What are the rules of the game? What does he see and hear at a basketball game? What does it feel like to score a basket? Declarative knowledge provided the information needed for the content of Paulo's story. Procedural knowledge provided Paulo with the strategies he would need for writing: How will the information on basketball be organized and presented in his writing? How will an interesting lead be crafted? How will effective transitions be written? How will paragraphs be constructed with correct capitalization, spelling, and punctuation? Procedural knowledge provided Paulo with an awareness of how to use specific writing strategies. Conditional knowledge provided him with the information needed for knowing when and why to apply specific strategies: When should he address writer's block, and what strategies does he have for overcoming the block? If a weakness can be identified in his writing, how does he address that weakness? When does he add or eliminate content from his writing? Why is this important? It became necessary for Paulo to tap into all three types of metacognitive knowledge. Each type was needed to guide effective writing performance. (For more resources on metacognitive knowledge, see Box 3.1.)

Box 3.1
Additional Resources on Metacognition

Borkowski, J.G. (1992). Metacognitive theory: A framework for teaching literacy, writing and math skills. *Journal of Learning Disabilities, 25*(4), 253–257.

Brown, A.L. (1980). Metacognitive development and reading. In R.J. Spiro, B.B. Bruce, & W.F. Brewer (Eds.), *Theoretical issues in reading comprehension* (pp. 453–481). Hillsdale, NJ: Erlbaum.

Palincsar, A.S. (1986). Metacognitive strategy instruction. *Exceptional Children, 53*(2), 118–124.

Palincsar, A.S., & Brown, D.A. (1987). Enhancing instructional time through attention to metacognition. *Journal of Learning Disabilities, 20*(2), 66–75.

Research provides evidence that the procedural and conditional knowledge of more skilled writers is more detailed, focused, and complex than that of students who struggle with the process of writing (Bereiter & Scardamalia, 1987). Struggling writers are often unaware of the strategies that more skilled writers use for planning, writing, revising, and problem solving. If they are aware, however, many do not recognize when or how to apply these strategies. The immature and ineffective writing strategies often used by struggling writers make the process of writing difficult (MacArthur & Graham, 1987; MacArthur, Graham, & Schwartz, 1991; Thomas et al., 1987). Pressley and Levin (1986) write, "Such learners use fewer strategies than do more proficient learners, and they use them less often and less effectively" (p. 179).

Harris and Graham (1992) suggest that struggling writers require more support with specific writing strategies, as well as instruction that guides their awareness of when and why to apply these strategies. Englert and Raphael (1989) also make a case for teaching writing strategies:

> If disabled writers exhibit less control of the writing process and are more dependent on external criteria and resources (e.g., teachers) than on their own internal resources, then strategy instruction must emphasize their writing procedures as well as develop students' knowledge of how to flexibly activate, adapt, and monitor the strategy in different writing circumstances. (p. 117)

*Reflection Point 3.1*_____

1. Take time to reflect in your journal on the writing strategies you use while writing. What prewriting strategies do you use? Drafting strategies? Revision strategies? Editing strategies? What do you do when you reach a stumbling block? What strategies do you use to overcome writing difficulties?

2. Interview another writer. Are his or her writing strategies similar to yours or different?

Scaffolding Writing Development

In this chapter, I will share some of the teacher-student interactions that took place in Kate's writing classroom. During these interactions, I wanted to scaffold learning by encouraging students to think strategically and maintain a problem-solving focus while writing. Wood, Bruner, and Ross (as cited in Rogoff & Lave, 1984) use the term *scaffold* as a metaphor to describe the ideal role of a teacher. When I think of a scaffold, I am reminded of the temporary platform my husband built while painting barns in the midwestern United States. He began painting the lower levels of the barn and slowly built a framework to go higher. Without the support of scaffolding, he would have been unable to reach the highest peak of the barn. According to Greenfield (1984),

> The scaffold, as it is known in building construction, has five characteristics: it provides support; it functions as a tool; it extends the range of the worker; it allows the worker to accomplish a task not otherwise possible; and it is used selectively to aid the worker where needed. (p. 118)

In the writing classroom, teachers can provide students the instructional scaffolding necessary to reach their highest potential as writers. Such support occurs by providing the right question or the right information at the right time. Greenfield (1984) writes, "Initially in the learning of language or other skills, the teacher carries the greatest responsibility in the activity, erecting a scaffold for the child's limited skills" (p. 117).

In Kate's classroom, scaffolding student learning often meant modeling desired writing behavior, and much of what I did with these writers involved modeling through talk. Through conversation with the four student writers, I tried to present new ideas and new ways of looking at their writing processes. I shared my experiences with writing, as well as my struggles and frustrations and ways I might get around them. I found myself demonstrating new ways to think about their writing process. During my conversations with the students, I always took into account the individual student's current strengths, weaknesses, and writing issues. I tried to pay close attention to the problems students were experiencing and catch them in the midst of their difficulties. These interactions helped me begin to better understand the experiences of struggling writers in a process-approach classroom.

I found myself continually challenged to find ways to scaffold writing, especially during drafting and revision. Asking questions was an effective way of directing and developing these stages of the writing process; this was especially helpful when I could model good questions and demonstrate for young writers how to ask *themselves* good questions. During drafting, I asked questions such as the following:

- What are you trying to say in this paragraph?
- What do you want your readers to know?
- What are your main thoughts?
- What details can you provide to support your thoughts?
- How can you best arrange your ideas?

The best questions created an interactive, problem-solving environment for us, and most were used to serve as a springboard for further discussion. For example, one day Daniel was stuck with his writing. He had an idea for his piece, but no direction for writing it. As I approached Daniel's desk, I saw a title, "The Graveyard." An idea was beginning to form, but Daniel had not yet found clear direction to his piece. To help develop his ideas, I tried to model the questions mature writers ask themselves when drafting a piece: Who was in the graveyard (main characters)? Why were they there, or what do they want to do? What exciting event will happen while they are in the graveyard? What happens next? How could you add some description to this scene?

During revision, questions once again became a springboard for interactions with the students. In another instance, Amy had just completed her first draft of "Grandfather's Pocket Watch." It was time to revise her piece so, using some of the following questions, I tried to engage Amy in the process of revision:

- What have you said so far?
- What have you been trying to say?
- How does it sound when you read it out loud?
- What is good about your draft that you can expand on?
- What is not so good that you could spend more time on?
- What will your readers think when they read this?
- What questions might they ask?

Scaffolding student writing using questions requires *listening* to what the writer is trying to say or do and building on their knowledge base. It requires *asking* the key questions that good writers might ask themselves when they write or revise, and it requires *engaging* the students in their own learning through conversation.

In the next sections, I will discuss some of the individual problems these four students experienced, and I will explain some of the strategies we used to overcome these obstacles.

Amy—Planning and Organizing a Piece

A common routine in many writing classrooms is for teachers to conference with students on completion of a written piece. I found it important also to meet with the students who struggled *before* they began writing. Spending time with them during the initial phases of writing prompted proactive teaching. It provided an opportunity to talk about their piece before they began to compose. This kind of conversation reinforced concepts learned during the previous writing period. It also helped to generate ideas and encouraged students to think ahead to specific writing tasks. By spending time with struggling writers before they begin writing, teachers can reinforce specific writing strategies appropriate to students' writing needs.

One afternoon, Amy greeted me with these words: "I'm stuck…I don't know what to write about next. Will you help me?" Our conversation began with a discussion about choosing a topic. "It can be a topic that you know a lot about, something that is important to you," I said.

Ms. C.:	What do you do after school, Amy?
Amy:	Nothing. I'm grounded.
Ms. C.:	What is something you know about that others might like to read about?
Amy:	I don't know. (long pause)
Ms. C.:	Your family?
Amy:	I already wrote about my sister.

Amy's body language sent a message to me: She did not think her life stories were very exciting. She did not think these stories provided the content needed for writing. Calkins (1994) writes,

> Our children's lives are brim full of concerns and stories, and yet when we ask them to write about their experiences they often say, "Nothing happens in my life".… When we help children know that their lives do matter, we are teaching writing (pp. 15–16).

How would I help Amy recognize that the "stuff" of her life was a great source for writing material? I once again was encouraged by Calkins's comments. In her book titled *The Art of Teaching Writing*, Calkins shares that she often pulled her chair alongside her students and listened carefully to their words. "You know so much," Calkins would say to her students. "What you are teaching me is amazing stuff. You need to tell this to the world. It's huge. It's so big. Write it down" (p. 15). With this in mind, Amy and I generated a list of topics relevant to her life:

- My Family
- My Friends
- Moving
- Winter Recess Fun
- Walking to School
- My Favorite Food

We inserted this list into Amy's writing workshop binder for future reference.

This time, Amy decided to write about moving, a topic she felt confident to write about. Amy wrote the title "When I Moved" at the top of her paper and immediately began writing, giving no thought to the content whatsoever. It was evident that Amy was beginning her writing with little advance planning. She approached the writing task by retrieving from memory whatever seemed appropriate and then quickly wrote it down. Very little reflection or planning was taking place.

"Amy, let's try something," I interjected. I wrote the word *Moving* in the center of her paper, and we began to create a story web of her thoughts (see Figure 8). As a strategy, story webbing can contribute significantly to idea generation. It also can help a writer add detail and organization to a piece. We first worked through the webbing strategy together so Amy could see how it worked. Amy watched closely as I guided our discussion and introduced a way to plan and organize her new piece about moving.

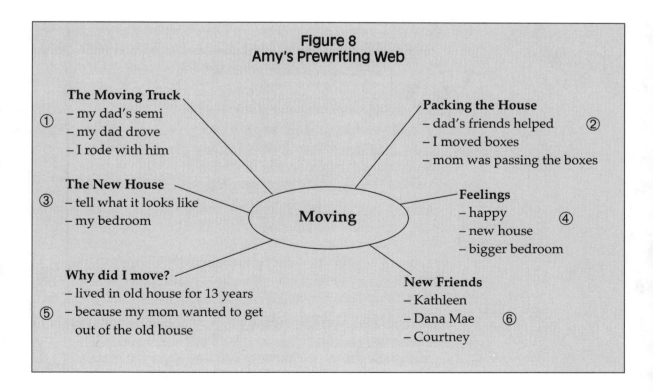

Figure 8
Amy's Prewriting Web

The Moving Truck
① – my dad's semi
– my dad drove
– I rode with him

Packing the House
– dad's friends helped ②
– I moved boxes
– mom was passing the boxes

The New House
③ – tell what it looks like
– my bedroom

Moving

Feelings
– happy ④
– new house
– bigger bedroom

Why did I move?
– lived in old house for 13 years
⑤ – because my mom wanted to get
   out of the old house

New Friends
– Kathleen
– Dana Mae ⑥
– Courtney

We talked about all the things she could write about her move, and then illustrated her ideas in a web. She described the contents of six categories: why she had to move, the moving truck, packing the house, the new house, her feelings, and her new friends. Amy then numbered these categories in the order in which she wanted to write about them. She added details to each category, which formed the basis for each paragraph in her piece. Amy began to understand the concept of paragraphing with this strategy for organizing writing.

Story webbing provided an opportunity for Amy to brainstorm and cluster her ideas. It also provided an opportunity for her to organize her writing by spending a few moments preplanning what she wanted to say. A map or plan for her writing had been developed, and she knew where her writing was heading next. She did not lose precious time reviewing, rethinking, reorganizing, or redoing. Further, webbing contributed to idea generation, and Amy's writing became more detailed. As Amy put it, "I'm getting lots of thoughts in my head. They keep coming and coming! Look how many ideas I have!"

Amy caught on very quickly to this strategy and began writing with a clear idea of her task in mind. She relied heavily on her story web during her writing process by using it to add, delete, and rearrange ideas. Only a few moments passed when she enthusiastically approached me and said, "When I started writing I just realized how much stuff I did when I moved." The story in Figure 9 is the result of Amy's efforts.

On completion of this story, Amy and I compared it with a story she previously had written.

Ms. C.:	What do you notice about your writing Amy?
Amy:	This story is longer...it's better...and it is more interesting.

This story was a beginning—the beginning of good things to come.

In Amy's next piece, which was about her family, she used this first story web as a model and followed similar steps. She was able to construct a web on her own successfully, describing more specifically this time each member of her family. Again, her story web became a guide for her writing. She referred to it regularly, checking off ideas and elaborating on

Figure 9
Amy's Story

Page 1

When I Moved

When I moved we had a
moveing tuck. It was my dad's semi
My dad drove. I rode with him.

Then my dad's friends helped. I
helped moving boxes. My mom was passing
the boxes over the fence.

The day before I moved my mom
bought some food and buns. Then my
cousin came and at with us.

My New house has rug in it. It has
two big bathrooms. My sisters room is
down stairs. My mom and dad have
a big bedroom. My sister has a big
room too. I have a big bedroom too
but my bed takes up the whole space

(continued)

Figure 9 (continued)
Amy's Story

Page 2

In my backyard I have a deck
and it has a roof.

I felt happy when I moved into
a house because I get a bigger
bedroom, and a bigger basement,
and bigger space.

I moved out of my old house
because we lived there for 13 years and
my mom wanted to get out of the old
house.

I moved in my new house because
my mom said, "let's buy a new house"
We rented my old house and we lived
in a duplex.

When I moved to a new school I
knew courtney before I came to

(continued)

Figure 9 (continued)
Amy's Story

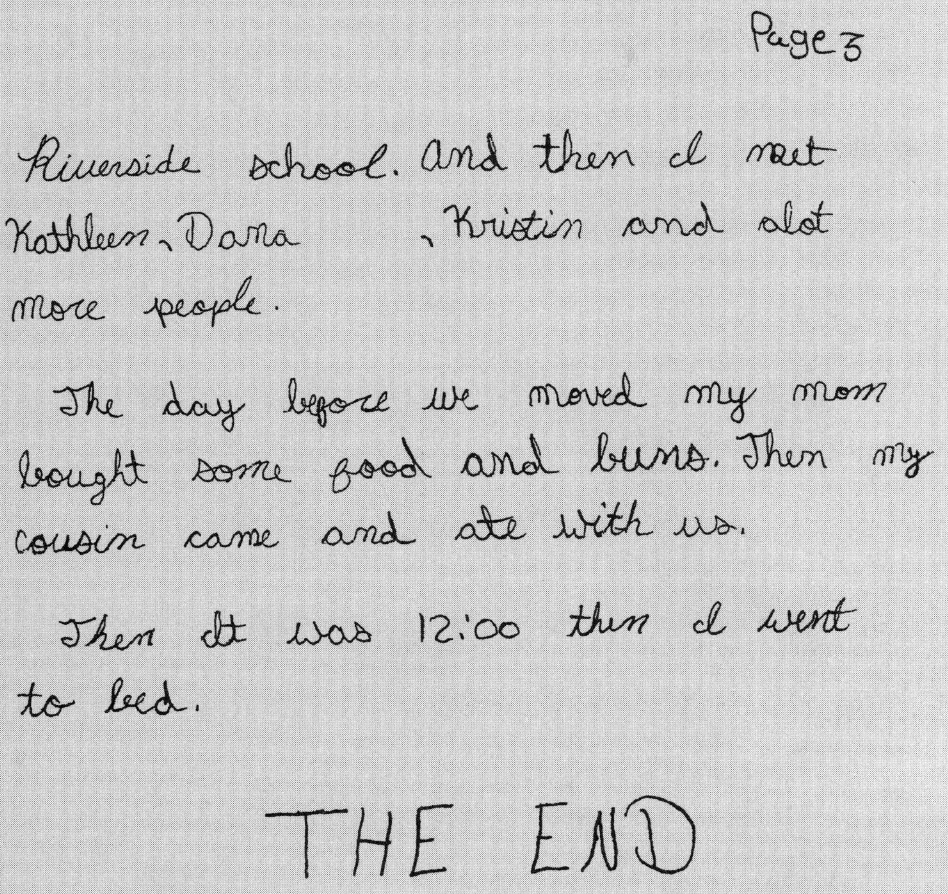

Page 3

Riverside school. And then I met Kathleen, Dana , Kristin and alot more people.

The day before we moved my mom bought some food and buns. Then my cousin came and ate with us.

Then it was 12:00 then I went to bed.

THE END

original thoughts. For Amy, story webbing helped to generate, organize, and expand on her ideas. After using the strategy, we were able to discuss how effective it was and why.

Ms. C.:   Why do you think that [your story web] helped with your writing?

Amy: 'Cuz it gives good ideas.

We talked about how to use the strategy in subsequent assignments. It was not long before Amy was taking control of the strategy herself. She even described in writing the process for creating her story web (see Figure 10).

Dialogue prompts "the kinds of opportunities necessary for the teacher to provide scaffolded instruction" (Palincsar, 1986b, p. 73). With Amy, it was through conversation that I nudged her from one level of competence to the next. Story webbing provided the scaffolding she needed to take on more challenging tasks. See Box 3.2 for more strategies to use to help students generate ideas.

Figure 10
Amy's Written Description of the Story Web Strategy

1. In the middle write your topic. Circle it.

2. Write ideas about your topic.

3. Write details about each idea.

4. Decide which idea goes first, second, third and fourth (or any number that you had on the story map).

5. Write an introduction.

6. Rough draft.

7. Write an Ending.

Box 3.2
Prewriting Strategies Used to Generate Ideas

Writers use a variety of prewriting strategies to generate ideas as they begin to write:

1. Freewriting—Young writers can write freely on a topic of their choice. They should be encouraged to write as quickly as possible without stopping. Freewriting for a specific amount of time often helps students break through writing blocks and allows time for ideas to surface.

2. Brainstorming—When young writers brainstorm, they quickly list everything that comes to mind on a specific topic. All student ideas should be recorded with little judgment or criticism from the teacher. The focus of brainstorming should remain on generating ideas.

3. Drawing—Drawing can be an effective technique to help students make use of their prior knowledge because it helps young writers formulate their ideas and retrieve details that may not surface immediately. Their artwork can also provide prompts for identifying what details to develop in their writing. Students can draw storyboards that illustrate characters, settings, events, and main ideas before composing their written pieces.

4. Researching—Often writers must gather information before they write. Researching begins after a topic has been chosen. Students refer to specific books and reference materials on their topic to gather background information.

5. Journaling—Journals can be written in a variety of forms. However, most include an author's ideas, questions, passions, and insights. Journals encourage young authors to reflect on their daily experiences and become more aware of what is happening in their lives.

6. Observing—Our world is full of ideas for writing. When students become careful observers of the world around them, they learn to "see" more. Encourage young writers to tune into familiar events of their lives to gain a deeper appreciation of their experiences and surroundings.

Kenda—Focusing on One Step at a Time and Fostering a Positive Attitude About Writing

For all students, writing is a complex process; therefore, it is easy for students to become entangled in many complicated issues all at once. Idea generation, word choice, finding a voice, organization, spelling, grammar, and handwriting are only a few of the issues writers must deal with at one time. For Kenda, the process of writing required the synthesis of many skills and abilities. This made writing difficult. To simplify the multiple challenges of writing, Kenda and I implemented the double-dictation strategy (Collins, 1998; see also Appendix C). With this strategy, I tried to ease the cognitive burden involved in the process of writing by breaking down Kenda's writing into three important steps: idea generation, writing, and revising/editing. We began our conversation by focusing on idea generation. I wrote down Kenda's story ideas as she dictated them to me, which allowed her to focus her energy on thinking. Together we generated story ideas during one writing period, and a thematic thread was maintained throughout her composition. The following dialogue provides a glimpse into our conversation on idea generation.

Ms. C.:	How's your writing going today, Kenda?
Kenda:	I'm thinking.
Ms. C.:	What are you thinking about?
Kenda:	My Chapter 2. I'm trying to write about what happened at my house last night.
Ms. C.:	Tell me. Tell me what happened.
Kenda:	Well...when I got home from school, my mom wasn't there.
Ms. C.:	Were you home all by yourself?
Kenda:	No. My brother was home. I don't like it when he babysits me. I want to babysit myself.
Ms. C.:	Tell me more.
Kenda:	Sometimes I just want to take care of myself. I am not a baby any more.
Ms. C.:	No, Kenda, you are not a baby anymore; you have grown into a beautiful young girl.
Kenda:	Yeah. My mom worries about what will happen if I'm home alone. She thinks a stranger might come.
Ms. C.:	Let's try and write about your thoughts. How about letting me write today? You can concentrate on telling your story.
Kenda:	OK.

Kenda then communicated her story ideas to me, and I wrote down her words exactly as spoken. This exchange produced the following story:

Just My Luck

I came home from school. I yelled, "Mom! Dad!" My brother answered, "Mom and Dad aren't home. I am supposed to baby-sit you."

"I don't need a baby-sitter. I am not a baby."

"Fine then. I'll leave you home alone."

Someone knocked on the door. I looked out the peep hole. It was the guy in the green van. I ran upstairs and then I started to panic. He rang the door bell. I did not answer the door. I felt worried and confused. I looked out the peep hole. "Oh, no." He is still there. I sat down. I thought to myself, "Now I do wish that my brother Andy was here!"

Kenda transferred her ideas from our conversation into her writing. During our dialogue, she was able to choose words carefully to describe the experience and to sequence her ideas into a story. We then moved the focus of Kenda's energy to writing. I dictated the story back to her while she wrote it down. I helped her with spelling or other questions when she requested assistance.

The final stage of this strategy involved comparing the two drafts to check for spelling and writing conventions:

Ms. C.:	Let's next compare your draft with my draft. Let's look at how the two drafts are alike and how they are different.

[Together, we compared the first sentence, "I came home from school." Kenda closely examined the spelling of each word and decided that her sentence looked good.]

Ms. C.:	You are right, Kenda. The spelling is just great. There are some other things, however, that authors also need to watch out for as they write. What else, besides spelling, will make this sentence easier for the reader to read?
Kenda:	Hmmm... [I point to the end of her sentence]
Kenda:	I might need a stop sign.
Ms. C.:	Yes, you need to add a period. A period tells the writer the sentence is over. It gives their mind and eyes a little break from reading.

Implementing this double-dictation strategy allowed Kenda an opportunity to focus on only one aspect of writing at a time. First, while I was writing, she focused on content generation. Then as I dictated the story back to her, she focused her energy on the physical task of handwriting. Finally, when the two drafts were compared, Kenda was able to concentrate only on revising and editing. This strategy broke the process of writing into manageable pieces for her, and nothing was left out. She gained

Figure 11
Kenda's Final Draft of "Just My Luck"

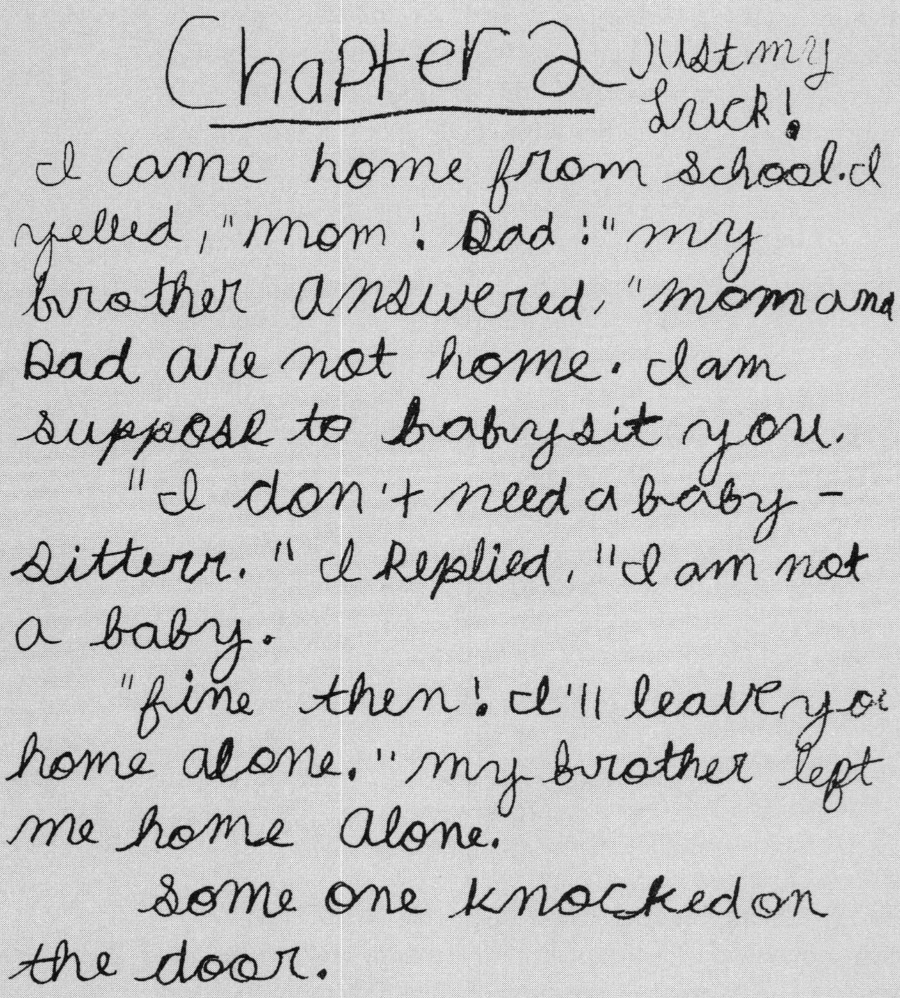

Chapter 2 Just my Luck!

I came home from school. I yelled, "Mom! Dad!" my brother answered, "mom and Dad are not home. I am suppose to babysit you.

"I don't need a baby-sitterr." I Replied, "I am not a baby.

"fine then! I'll leave you home alone." my brother left me home alone.

some one knocked on the door.

experience with prewriting, generating content, writing, and editing. Figure 11 shows the beginning of her final draft.

From this experience, Kenda could begin to see her own progress and success. Her writing began to look like *real* writing, and she began sharing her piece with peers. This particular piece evolved chapter by chapter. Kenda took pride in her progress, and her writing fluency slowly began to increase. By focusing on only one aspect of her written piece at a time, Kenda had less chance of becoming overwhelmed or frustrated.

Collins (1998), for example, presents copying strategies as commonplace in the growth and development of most learners. Struggling writers often refer to these strategies when writing gets difficult. Appendix C provides additional information on Collins's work as well as his writing strategies.

When I looked at Kenda's written work, I often saw the chance to address several writing strategies at once. Her writing was filled with many places from which to begin instruction. Early on, I found myself tempted to talk about too many concepts at once. As I became more comfortable with her, I tried to focus our conversations on the one difficulty that mattered the most at that particular time. With Kenda, it became important to talk about only one idea per piece. By focusing on one difficulty, she could concentrate on a single task and begin to experience success.

As I reflect, I also recall the tensions I experienced many times as I pulled my chair alongside Kenda's desk. I learned something valuable: Our instructional efforts become fruitless if we do not first give consideration to the writing environment created in the classroom and students' attitudes toward writing. When only a few moments were available, I often had a choice to make between a focus on writing instruction or a focus on the development of a positive attitude toward writing. With this sensitive writer, promoting a positive attitude toward writing became a top priority. My decision was always made "in the moment." I followed my intuition based on Kenda's emotions at the time—her body language, mood, frustration level, and attitude. These split-second decisions had a profound effect on our relationship and helped to create a learning environment where Kenda felt appreciated and capable of learning. The vignette that follows shows this type of decision making in action.

I pulled my chair up next to Kenda, and I noticed right away that her paper contained a number of mechanical errors, but I had only a few moments to devote to her piece. The question came to mind: Shall I focus on reviewing spelling, capitalization, and punctuation, or shall I spend a few moments having fun with her written ideas?

Kenda read her piece out loud to me:

I have a band. Calld the Blosumse This summre we wint to nastkric and we sane at nastkric and me and lasale made. Fand sep braclit and nacklasis and we made tehs thins. That gow in your hare and at nastkric we wint bote ridin.

[I have a band called The Blossoms. This summer we went to Nest Creek and we sang at Nest Creek. And me and LaSalle made friendship bracelets and necklaces. And we made the things that go in your hair. And at Nest Creek we went boat riding.]

I decided to make positive comments and compliment her on her creative thoughts. We laughed because I told her that I once had a band too, although we were called "The Sisters."

I wonder, though, should I have spent the time helping Kenda with her spelling and placing periods at the end of every sentence? Or was I right to smile, laugh, giggle, and have some fun reflecting on our common past?

In this instance, top priority was given to fostering a positive attitude toward writing. At times, it was important for us just to have fun with Kenda's ideas. These moments validated her thoughts and encouraged her writing. Heathington (1994) writes,

> When forced to make a choice between promoting positive attitudes or emphasizing skill development, teachers seem to choose skill development. Their practices indicate they believe that skills are more essential for their students than the attitudes their students have toward literacy. (p. 199)

In order to view writing as a positive experience, students—especially those who struggle—benefit when surrounded by fun and rewarding writing moments. There are moments when we can choose to step back, relax, and allow time for a smile amidst the writing activity.

I often wondered if a focus on attitude and affect would impede skill development. Throughout this classroom research experience, I came to believe the opposite to be true. When energy for writing increased, Kenda's involvement with the process increased. The more she wrote, the more practice she received in developing written skills. Therefore, the affective domain can be seen as a central and guiding focus of writing instruction for struggling writers.

Daniel—Overcoming Mechanical Challenges, Especially Spelling

For struggling writers who have not yet mastered the mechanical aspects of written language, attending to these lower level skills can become an important part of their writing instruction (Graham & Harris, 1988). Contends Graham (1992),

> It is important for students to develop enough fluency so that the mechanics of writing don't cause them to forget ideas already developed, interfere with intentions or plans at the point of translation, or disrupt planning about the next unit of text to be written. (p. 140)

Within a workshop environment, writing provides a vehicle for learning about capitalization, punctuation, grammar, and conventional spelling. Development of these mechanical skills can take place within the context of students' real writing.

For Daniel, conventional spelling was particularly problematic. In this writing workshop classroom, correct spelling was not an issue during the early stages of writing. It was necessary, however, that misspellings be corrected for final and published drafts. Students were expected to self-edit their own writing for misspellings. This self-edit was followed by a peer edit, and then handed to a teacher for a final response. Daily interactions with Daniel prompted me to wonder, How would I help him with his spelling within the context of his own writing? As Graves (1983) writes, "Spelling is for writing. Children may achieve high scores on phonics inventories, or weekly spelling tests. But the ultimate test is what the child does under 'game conditions,' within the process of moving toward meaning" (pp. 193–194). I felt it necessary to help Daniel develop some of the writing strategies used by skilled spellers in the midst of their writing process. This was important to him because he wanted to communicate effectively with his peers through writing. Daniel told me, "I just want my paper to look right, so other kids can read it."

Bear, Invernizzi, Templeton, and Johnston (2000) encourage teachers to spend time exploring words throughout the school day. When we closely examine the words in our surroundings, we can point out minor variations in words, compare and contrast words, or pay attention to what remains the same in words. By doing this on a regular basis, we encourage learners to expand their knowledge of spelling patterns. Henderson writes, "Those who learn how to 'walk through' words with sensible expectations, noting sound, pattern, and meaning relationships, will know what to remember, and they will learn to spell English" (as cited in Ganske, 2000, p. 2). In other words, when writers become able to identify spelling consistencies, they will then be able to generalize their learnings to other words, and learn to write and spell more efficiently.

Daniel and I first established a place in his workshop binder where he could write down the high-frequency words he used regularly in his writing. This was a place he could refer to for correct spellings as he wrote. He titled this page "Words I Use a Lot in My Writing." His list grew each week and included words from his writing such as *when, with, went, those, weren't, again,* and *there.* We then included a second page to document unique and more complex words that were particularly troublesome for Daniel. He titled this page "Other Spelling Words." Again, this list evolved from Daniel's writing and included words such as *years, around, ears, catch, broke, replied, decide,* and *suppose.*

One day, Daniel and I noticed that two of the words on his "Other Spelling Words" list were similar: *years* and *ears.* With these words in mind, we tried to brainstorm a whole collection of similar words. He added *rears, hears, nears, tears, fears,* and *gears* to this list. All of these words produced the same "ears" spelling pattern. We also identified two words that did not quite fit this spelling pattern: *mirrors* and *peers.* We labeled these words with a question mark. This quick word study suggested to Daniel that he could turn to other similar words and spelling patterns when trying to spell troublesome words. When spellers approach a word they do not know how to spell, they often ask themselves, "What other similar words do I know that may help me here?"

I then examined the trends that were revealed within Daniel's misspellings. Examining his invented spellings revealed a few customary error patterns. I found that a high percentage of his misspelled words were spelled phonetically:

- "agen" for *again*
- "picketd" for *picked*
- "alamanum" for *aluminum*
- "riplied" for *replied*
- "desided" for *decided*
- "thows" for *those*
- "cach" for *catch*
- "thar" for *there*
- "ceper" for *keeper*
- "brote" for *brought*
- "frendes" for *friends*

Whenever Daniel tried to spell phonetically, incorrect spellings resulted. So I asked him, "What do you do when you don't know how to spell a word in your writing?" Daniel replied, "I write it the best I can."

It became apparent that Daniel was relying only on "sounding out" each troublesome word. Inventing spelling is one strategy for spelling unfamiliar words. However, Daniel also needed to learn to rely on visual memory for the correct spelling of many words. Therefore, instead of always requesting that Daniel "sound out" a problematic word, I would ask him, "Do you remember what the word looks like? Try and picture the word in your mind. What do you see?" With these questions, we worked toward developing Daniel's visual memory.

Helping Daniel examine the words found in his own writing was one way to support and extend his spelling development. It also became important for him to develop the skills of a proofreader. Proofreading requires careful attention while reading and prompts students to locate misspelled words in their writing.

Daniel did not have a clear strategy for identifying and correcting misspelled words in his writing; he simply wrote them the best way he knew how and then waited for a peer or teacher to correct them, abdicating responsibility for editing his spelling mistakes to his friends and the adults in the classroom. In my conferences with Daniel, I encouraged him to use his own resources to find a means for solving his spelling problems.

I first asked Daniel to identify any words in his writing that "didn't look right" when proofreading. I wanted him to learn to flag possible misspellings in his own writing. This was not easy: Daniel did not have the kind of visual awareness that makes misspelled words jump out, so he could not always identify his spelling errors. There would be times when he would overlook misspelled words and other times when he would flag words that were spelled correctly. In time, however, Daniel learned to trust his feelings and his visual memory. If he thought a word did not look right, there was a good chance it was misspelled.

Once he located a misspelled word, I asked Daniel to identify the *part* of the word that did not look right. Was it the beginning, the middle, or the end of the word? I wanted him to focus on the troublesome spot. I tried to guide Daniel's thinking and confirm or help with the final spelling. When the correct spelling was identified, I asked questions that encouraged him to think about how he made those decisions: How did you know that? Why do you think it works that way?

This was an attempt to help Daniel come up with correct spellings on his own, while modeling the thought processes of proficient spellers. I wanted Daniel to begin to think for himself rather than turn to an outside authority for correct spellings. (For more strategies to use with struggling spellers, see the resources listed in Box 3.3.)

Box 3.3
Resources for Word Study

Bear, D.R., Invernizzi, M., Templeton, S., & Johnston, F. (2000). *Words their way: Word study for phonics, vocabulary, and spelling instruction*. Englewood Cliffs, NJ: Prentice-Hall.

Ganske, K. (2000). *Word journeys: Assessment-guided phonics, spelling, and vocabulary instruction*. New York: Guilford.

Paulo—Finding the Motivation to Write

I began to recognize the small steps of growth that were occurring in Kenda, Amy, and Daniel. Through all of this sat Paulo. Each day I would check in with him, only to receive a cold shoulder or awkward silence. I found myself unconsciously avoiding this writer because it was so difficult to communicate with him. The following dialogue is typical of our beginning conversations:

| **Ms. C.:** | Hi, Paulo. How's your writing going today? |
| **Paulo:** | Fine. |

[I notice only his name is written at the top of his paper.]

Ms. C.:	Have you decided what you are going to write about next?
Paulo:	No. I don't want to write.
Ms. C.:	I would be happy to help you brainstorm some possible topics for your piece.
Paulo:	I don't want to do this. I don't want to write.

Helping Paulo required a great deal of energy on my part. My journal entry reflects my frustration:

> To communicate requires input from BOTH conversation participants...our conversations are limited. How much energy shall I expend to try and crack this tough exterior? Will I ever be able to talk to Paulo about his writing?

Teaching and learning requires a collaborative effort between both teacher and student. It requires that teachers support students through conversation and questioning, and it also requires that students take ownership for their learning and become actively involved in the process (Cambourne, 1995). For Paulo to grow as a writer, he first needed to become engaged as a writer. I could see that helping Paulo move ahead in his writing would require some kind of a connection between the two of us. I began looking for every opportunity to personally connect with this young writer.

> *One day, Paulo was stuck. He did not seem to know what to do next. He had no further ideas for his story. Conversation had not worked well with Paulo in the past. He was never interested in talking about his ideas while he wrote. I tried again, but our conversation went nowhere.*

During the silence between the two of us, Paulo began admiring my mechanical pencil. I am not sure why I did this, or where this explanation came from, but I explained that it was a magic pencil filled with many great ideas for stories. "Would you like to write with it, Paulo?" His brown eyes became quite large. We exchanged pencils, my blue mechanical pencil for his one-inch stump. He began writing furiously. Once he started, he did not stop. His story grew and grew.

After class, he approached me to return the pencil. I asked him if he wanted to keep it as a special pencil meant only for writing amazing stories. Again, his large eyes lit up. I could detect a small smile hidden there somewhere. Paulo carefully tucked the pencil away safely in his writing workshop binder.

While putting on his winter coat, Paulo asked, "Are you sure I can keep the special pencil?"

"Yes, Paulo," I responded

While putting on his boots, he asked, "Do you want it back next week?"

"No, Paulo."

Walking out the door he said, "Thanks for the pencil."

"You are welcome."

Paulo talked to me!

This is the moment I recall when we connected. It did not involve a specific writing strategy or a well-planned lesson. The simple act of exchanging pencils initiated a different atmosphere between the two of us. Once this occurred, questions began surfacing in my mind about how to continue connecting with Paulo. What influences had led Paulo toward becoming a disengaged writer? What experiences had affected his attitudes toward writing? What conditions would need to be established for him to begin the task of writing each day? How could the atmosphere within this classroom be redesigned to continue to foster positive writing motivations for Paulo?

Cambourne (1995) provides a framework that helped me think about Paulo's behavior. He describes eight conditions or prerequisites needed for learning to occur in the literacy classroom: immersion, demonstration, engagement, expectations, responsibility, approximations, employment, and response (see Figure 12).

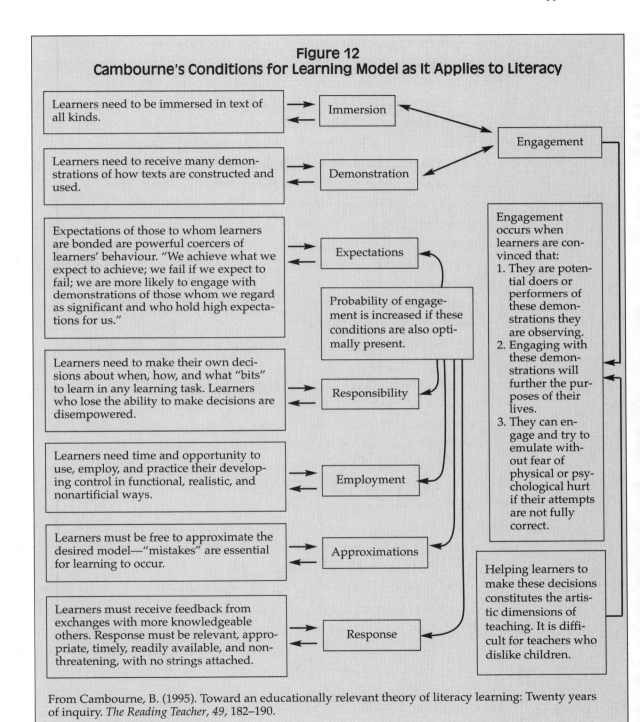

Figure 12
Cambourne's Conditions for Learning Model as It Applies to Literacy

Learners need to be immersed in text of all kinds. → Immersion

Learners need to receive many demonstrations of how texts are constructed and used. → Demonstration

Expectations of those to whom learners are bonded are powerful coercers of learners' behaviour. "We achieve what we expect to achieve; we fail if we expect to fail; we are more likely to engage with demonstrations of those whom we regard as significant and who hold high expectations for us." → Expectations

Learners need to make their own decisions about when, how, and what "bits" to learn in any learning task. Learners who lose the ability to make decisions are disempowered. → Responsibility

Learners need time and opportunity to use, employ, and practice their developing control in functional, realistic, and nonartificial ways. → Employment

Learners must be free to approximate the desired model—"mistakes" are essential for learning to occur. → Approximations

Learners must receive feedback from exchanges with more knowledgeable others. Response must be relevant, appropriate, timely, readily available, and nonthreatening, with no strings attached. → Response

Engagement

Probability of engagement is increased if these conditions are also optimally present.

Engagement occurs when learners are convinced that:
1. They are potential doers or performers of these demonstrations they are observing.
2. Engaging with these demonstrations will further the purposes of their lives.
3. They can engage and try to emulate without fear of physical or psychological hurt if their attempts are not fully correct.

Helping learners to make these decisions constitutes the artistic dimensions of teaching. It is difficult for teachers who dislike children.

From Cambourne, B. (1995). Toward an educationally relevant theory of literacy learning: Twenty years of inquiry. *The Reading Teacher, 49,* 182–190.

Reading Cambourne (1995) reminded me that engagement in a learning activity depends on a range of different behaviors. First, learners must be willing and able to attend to classroom demonstrations. For Paulo, this meant listening closely and learning from the instructions and minilessons provided by Kate throughout the workshop period. It also meant that he needed to be willing to attend to our conversations and learn from the dialogue that resulted. However, for Paulo, there was no perceived need or purpose for learning from this instruction.

His body language often sent subtle messages to me, asking, Where is the value in learning to write? Guthrie and Wigfield (1997) point out that valuing the task of writing may be one of the most important predictors of writing engagement. And as Cambourne (1995) writes, "Engagement also depends on active participation by the learner, which in turn involves some risk taking; learners can participate actively only if they are prepared to 'have a go'" (p. 185). Paulo and other struggling writers are often inhibited by attempts to write. Engaging in writing is risky because it involves putting your personal thoughts on paper and then having those personal thoughts made available for all to read. For those students who find writing difficult, risk taking becomes complicated. Writing risks are often met with critical opinions, corrections, or substitutions, which all provide further evidence of the writer's specific weaknesses. Confident writers, on the other hand, are often more willing to "put their work out there." Their writing can engage others in a more positive dialogue, thus reinforcing their writing development. In the writing classroom, it becomes important for teachers to receive the writing of struggling writers with enthusiasm and support. For writing growth to occur, writers must feel free to make mistakes and work toward approximations.

As stated in Chapter 2, although other struggling writers have very different instructional needs, they all tend to display an insecurity about themselves as writers. Their vulnerability easily opens them to criticism. Graham and Harris (1988) observe, "Intensive evaluation may make students more aware of their limitations and less willing to write, resulting in poorer writing performance" (p. 511). How teachers respond to young writers and their writing makes a tremendous difference in students' motivation to write. For me, there was no greater challenge than

responding to Paulo, this insecure and apprehensive writer who frequently had negative self images about his ability as an author.

Calkins (1994) writes, "Our decisions must be guided by what might
help this *writer* rather than what might help this *writing*" (p. 228). Throughout my time with Paulo, special care was given not to overemphasize error. Instead, every effort was made to provide supportive feedback that
encouraged improvement. It became important to *unconditionally* accept
his writing as his best work, remaining careful not to send implicit messages that his work was not adequate.

While working with Paulo, I also wanted to make visible the inner
dialogue that writers use during writing. It became important for him to
understand that writers talk to themselves. This inner dialogue may include a discussion on where they are, where they need to go, what needs
to get done to accomplish their writing goal, why something is or is not
working, or how well they are progressing. This self-talk is not intended
for communication with others. Most of this running dialogue helps writers orient themselves, organize their writing, and structure their writing
behavior. Writers essentially tell themselves what to do when they write.

Students can be taught to use self-speech called *self-instructions* to
regulate their writing behavior. Self-instructions are aimed at helping students understand the task of writing, produce effective writing strategies, monitor their writing process, and reward themselves for progress
made. What writers say to themselves and how they say it can either help
or hurt their process of writing. Harris and Graham (1996a) emphasize
the importance of self-instruction for the struggling writer. (See Appendix
B for examples of Harris and Graham's six basic types of self-instructions.)

A focus on self-instruction became an important part of my interactions with Paulo. As an example, Paulo was never quite sure of what to
do at the beginning of each writing period. He would open his workshop binder, which contained past and present work, and simply remain
seated, fiddling in his desk or talking to a friend. Paulo would not take
action toward writing progress. I approached his desk each day and
cheerfully asked, "Paulo, what are you up to today? What do you plan to
do?" These questions encouraged him to formulate a response and take
action. With modeling, repetition, and time, Paulo began to ask himself
these questions at the beginning of each writing period.

During our interactions, I also tried to model self-reinforcement for Paulo. Simply stated, self-reinforcement occurs when students choose to reinforce themselves for a job well done. For self-reinforcement to occur, it must be done free of any other external influences, such as teacher or parent. The young students themselves must use positive self-statements such as "Awesome!" "That was my best job!" or "I have just worked really hard!" as a reward for performance. To be most effective, the reinforcement must come from within the writer.

I found that self-reinforcement came very easily to some young writers. For Paulo, however, these skills needed to be taught through discussion and modeling. I found myself asking Paulo questions such as, What do you like about what you have written so far? What aspect of writing is getting easier for you? Don't you think the class would enjoy hearing what you have written so far? Aren't you proud of your accomplishments? Each interaction encouraged Paulo to think positively about his writing and provided verbal rewards for his work. In the midst of my modeling, I also wanted Paulo to begin to think about self-reinforcing his own writing. I asked, "What can you say to yourself that will make you proud of your work? Make sure you tell yourself what a good job you have done." I wanted Paulo to begin to become aware of the things he was saying to himself while writing.

Harris and Graham (1996) remind us that self-instructions are most effective when they are developed in the student's own words. Matching self-instruction to the student's verbal style and language helps to ensure that there will be a correspondence between saying and doing. It is important that "the student is not merely the passive recipient of the self-instructions and behaviors modeled, but rather plays an active, collaborative role in the design, implementation, and evaluation of self-instructions" (Harris & Graham, 1992, p. 91).

Reflection Point 3.2

In your journal, reflect on what you say to yourself while writing. How do you communicate with yourself when you are in the midst of a writing project? What do you say? How does this self-speech direct your writing behavior?

As Kate and I interacted with the young writers in this fifth-grade classroom, we were repeatedly reminded of the importance of keeping kids in sight. Each writing period provided new opportunities for us to help students empower themselves as writers and as learners. Dillon (2000) writes, "the students and events in our classroom that seem ordinary are not. All contributions, comments, actions, and interactions have meaning and share who we are and where we are headed in life. Each day is enlightening" (p. 156). Each day in this classroom prompted Kate and me to engage in self-exploration and reflect on our teaching practices. This process encouraged us to glean insights from our students and seek to identify specific ways to make the writing process clearer to young writers. In the next chapter, we will explore the process of learning to think strategically in the writing classroom. As strategic thinkers, teachers and students can learn to maintain a problem-solving focus while writing.

Chapter 4

Constructing Writing Strategies With Learners

Over the 5 months we were together, the four young writers with whom I worked in Kate's classroom assembled lists of specific writing strategies unique to each of them. These writing strategies were co-constructed through dialogue, within the context of the students' own writing, in response to each learner's specific writing difficulties. Collins (1998) uses the term *co-construction* to refer to the interactive dialogue that occurs between student and teacher. This term avoids "any attempt to simply give strategies to struggling writers, or to otherwise superimpose our strategies on their writing efforts" (p. 48). Figure 13 shows Kenda's, Paulo's, Daniel's, and Amy's lists of strategies.

Integrating Strategy Instruction and Process in the Elementary Writing Classroom

The process movement has represented a turning away from the traditional form of instruction. Process teaching and constructivism assume that students will develop their own writing abilities through the construction of knowledge for themselves. It is assumed that students will naturally acquire the ability to write through experiences with reading and writing. The role of the teacher is to support writing development rather than initiate, shape, or lead it.

In recent years, the process approach has been viewed by many as based on indirect rather than direct methods of instruction (Graham &

Figure 13
Students' Co-Constructed Writing Strategies

Kenda's Strategies for Writing

1. While writing a rough draft, I can focus on getting my ideas down on paper. Later, during editing, spelling and punctuation can be fixed up.

2. There is no need to spend time erasing on a rough draft. It is faster to cross out any changes I want to make.

3. In the FINAL draft I want to make sure words are spelled correctly. When copying the correct spelling of a word, I try and "take a picture" of the whole word. Then I copy the whole word. Copying words letter by letter is hard to do.

Paulo's Strategies for Writing

1. Choose a topic I am interested in. This makes writing more fun and meaningful. Writers want to put time and effort into pieces that are important to them.

2. Brainstorm a list of possible topics by writing down any idea I think I might be interested in. Choose the one that interests me the most. Save the list and add to it any time.

3. There are many things I can do to overcome writer's block. I can talk about my ideas with others. By talking, I can brainstorm new thoughts and new ways of thinking about my work. I can also think about my ideas throughout the day. Some of my best ideas come to me while walking to school, eating breakfast, and playing outside.

4. When I self-edit my writing, I check
   • to see if my writing makes sense by reading the story out loud;
   • punctuation (periods, commas, question marks, quotation marks);
   • capital letters; and
   • word spellings—I underline words that I am not sure how to spell.

Daniel's Strategies for Writing

1. I can take a few moments BEFORE writing to plan and organize my piece. This makes the writing easier for the reader to follow and enjoy.

2. Brainstorm ideas for a piece before beginning to write. Ideas for writing grow when I spend time thinking about them.

3. When I don't know how to spell a word in a rough draft, I can spell it the best way I know how and then underline it. After all my thoughts and ideas are written down, I can go back and check the spellings I am unsure of.

4. When I write, I can expect to have good days and bad days. On those days when writing is tough and it is hard to think of ideas, TALK TO A FRIEND. Talking with friends can give me good ideas for pieces. Talking helps organize my thinking.

(continued)

Figure 13 (continued)
Students' Co-Constructed Writing Strategies

5. Ideas for my writing can come from many places. Sometimes the best stories come from my experiences. I can think about what I have done, and the ideas will just come. I can also get good ideas from the books I read. Reading teaches me a lot about writing.

6. Try and find my own misspellings in my writing:
   - Find the words that "don't look just right."
   - Underline misspellings. (Trust your feelings. If you think a word doesn't look right, there is a good chance it is misspelled.)
   - Find the part of the word that doesn't look right. Is it the beginning, the middle, or the end? Zero in on that spot.
   - Try different ways of spelling the word. Do any of these look right?

Amy's Strategies for Writing

1. Take a few moments BEFORE writing to plan and organize a piece. This makes writing easier.

2. I should imagine what my writing will look like. How many paragraphs are needed? Does it have a title? An introduction? An ending?

3. Sometimes I might need to do research before I write. This means my piece needs more information. Interviewing family members can give me good information for my writing.

4. I can use descriptive words in my writing. This makes my piece interesting and fun for the reader. It helps the reader put a picture in their mind of what I am trying to say.

5. I can get great ideas for writing from my family experiences. Whenever I go on a family adventure I get ideas for writing.

6. When I get stuck, I just think my hardest. I think back and keep thinking. Ideas come.

It is important to note that the strategies co-constructed with these four children were strategies that encouraged them to *think*. The strategies did not provide the answer to their writing challenges. Instead, the strategies helped them to develop ways to solve their own writing problems.

Harris, 1996b). It has been criticized for leaving children on their own, learning to write without needed teacher intervention (Pressley & Woloshyn, 1995). Skeptics have been concerned that the methods used by process-approach teachers have not been powerful enough to help some students learn the knowledge, skills, or strategies needed to write adequately (Mather, 1992). Other critics of the process approach have argued that primary instructional emphasis has been placed on meaning and process, not form (see Delpit, 1988).

In the past, strategic writing instruction has been attacked for failing to fall within the constructivist perspective (Poplin, 1988). Some educators believe that constructivism and strategic instruction are incompatible (DuCharme, Earl, & Poplin, 1989). Many constructivists argue that strategy instruction does not allow for the students' own construction of knowledge. These educators view strategy instruction as telling students what to do. They believe this approach expects students to memorize steps or procedures and places the teacher in the role of expert manager or controller of the content. Learners have been characterized as passive, working on subskills they do not understand or care about. DuCharme and colleagues (1989) have argued that educators should abandon strategy instruction.

Many of these arguments equate strategy instruction with the traditional approach to teaching and learning that has dominated education for most of the century. Harris and Pressley (1991), however, suggest that "such conceptualization and descriptions of cognitive strategy instruction are inaccurate" (p. 393). Missing from these arguments by constructivists is an understanding of the interactive nature of strategic instruction. Good strategy instruction has the potential to encompass all the principles of constructivism and more.

Spiegel (1992) believes that bridges can be built between constructivist programs—such as process writing—and skill-oriented strategy instruction, and that combining indirect and direct methods of instruction "enables teachers to blend the best of both in order to help every child reach his or her literacy potential" (p. 43). Lensmire's (1994a) ethnographic research in a third-grade writing workshop also calls for balance between absolute teacher control and complete student autonomy. He has emphasized that teacher intervention and guidance are key to successful implementation of writing workshops. (See Box 4.1 for further reading on Lensmire's research, which takes a critical look at the theory and practice of writing workshops.) Balancing skills and processes in writing instruction may be an important component in improving the writing of struggling students (Collins, 1998; Graham & Harris, 1994; Harris & Graham, 1996a, 1996b; MacArthur, Schwartz, et al., 1991).

Recent research has further shown that strategy instruction embedded within a process approach can help achieve a balance in the

---

Box 4.1
Further Reading on Timothy Lensmire's Research

Lensmire, T.J. (1994a). *When children write: Critical re-visions of the writing workshop.* New York: Teachers College Press.

Lensmire, T.J. (1994b). Writing workshop as carnival: Reflections on an alternative learning environment. *Harvard Educational Review,* 64(4), 371–391.

Lensmire, T.J. (1997). *Powerful writing, responsible teaching.* New York: Teachers College Press.

---

development of skills and process (Collins, 1998; Englert, 1990; Harris & Graham, 1992; MacArthur, Schwartz, et al., 1991). Such a balanced approach encourages teachers to "think strategically about writing and the teaching of writing so that they can help writers identify and use strategies to control their own writing skills and writing processes" (Collins, 1998, p. vii). With strategic writing instruction, teachers use strategies to help students learn how to solve writing problems. In other words, "The goal of strategy instruction is to teach students to carry out independently the planning, writing, and revising processes that underlie effective writing" (MacArthur, Schwartz, et al., 1991, p. 234).

For some students, writing strategies are acquired intuitively from experience with reading and writing. Conversely, other students may require more specific support and guidance. For students who do not develop writing strategies naturally, strategic writing instruction can provide the needed support and practice necessary to help them overcome difficulties with writing (Collins, 1998; Harris & Graham, 1992).

The debate continues over whether we should teach writing skills or writing processes to help less skilled writers. Amidst this debate, we have looked at these options as if they have existed separately; that is, "We embraced these options one at a time, as if writing skills and writing processes could not possibly have anything to do with each other" (Collins, 1998, p. vii). However, "many precepts of constructivism have existed as part of cognitive strategy instruction since its inception" (Harris & Pressley, 1991, p. 394). Good strategy instruction places emphasis on the interactive and collaborative role of the learner. Strategy instruction can keep students actively involved in the construction of writing strategies. The teacher can "provide the conditions through which the child can discover for himself what strategies to employ" (Meichenbaum, as cited in Harris & Pressley, 1991, p. 394).

Furthermore, strategic writing instruction can be tailored to the needs of individual students. Strategies are constructed by students to fit their personal learning styles and needs (Swanson, 1989). A match between the strategy and the learner is characteristic of strategic instruction. Effective strategic writing instruction does not apply strategies in isolation from the person, process, or context.

Finally, "good strategic writing instruction is not rote. Students are not just memorizing steps and mechanically executing them; strategy instructors are not drill sergeants" (Harris & Pressley, 1991, p. 401). Rather, good strategy instruction involves making students aware of when, how, and why strategies work. Teachers are responsive to students' needs and collaborate with them in an interactive learning environment.

New directions in process-writing instruction are bringing a changing focus to the field of teaching. New ways of thinking about writing workshops are prompting teachers to explore new practices within process pedagogy. Current research suggests that strategy instruction fits well into a process-approach classroom (Collins, 1998; Collins & Collins, 1996; Danoff, Harris & Graham, 1993; Harris & Graham, 1992) because strategies can be presented to individual writers through conferences or to entire classes through minilessons.

Strategic writing instruction and process-based writing both have the same goal: improve student writing. In a writing workshop environment, students choose their own topics, determine the content and purpose of their writing, and select pieces for publication. In this classroom setting, strategies can be constructed within the context of students' own writing and are not applied in isolation. Individualizing instruction while students are in the middle of their writing process is the best time to discover strategies that will assist their writing development (Freedman, 1987). Current research demonstrates that strategy instruction can be successfully integrated into the current process approach to writing. Write Danoff and colleagues (1993), "Incorporating strategy instruction into a process approach to writing can meaningfully augment students' composition skills" (p. 319).

Helping students to think carefully and strategically about their writing process is the goal of strategy instruction in a process-approach classroom. It is important to remember, however, that no single set of strategies will provide the right approach for all students at any given time. The writing needs of individual students will vary, therefore strategy choice will vary. No one specific set of strategies will address the complexity of writing problems that exist within a writing classroom (Harris & Graham, 1996a). As a result, it is important for teachers to become familiar with a wide range of writing strategies. With this broad foundation, teachers can identify and present specific writing strategies to individuals, small groups of students, or the entire class as needed.

To develop my own framework for strategy instruction, I chose to explore and learn from several different validated writing strategies. I looked at those strategies that were grounded in current theories of writing process. Three groups of researchers emerged who provided the foundation I needed to begin thinking strategically in the writing classroom:

1. Carol Sue Englert and colleagues—Cognitive Strategy Instruction in Writing (CSIW) (See Appendix A.)

2. Karen R. Harris and Steve Graham—Strategies for Composition and Self-Regulation (See Appendix B; see also Chapter 3.)

3. James L. Collins—Strategic Writing Instruction (See Appendix C.)

The examples presented in Appendixes A, B, and C should be viewed amidst a range of possibilities for teachers to begin to think strategically about their students' writing. Samples of existing strategies have been provided to be used as *starting points* in the development and co-construction of new writing strategies because the goal of strategic writing instruction is for teachers and students to begin to think strategically about writing as they come together to co-construct personally meaningful strategies that will assist writers in overcoming specific writing difficulties. In this way, strategy instruction can help writers plan, shape, and control their writing.

Building Strategies Together

Palincsar (1986a) uses the metaphor of a football game to describe strategy instruction. Football teams have a variety of strategies or game plans they can use at a moment's notice. During a game, a football team must select the strategy that best fits the situation at the moment. Members of the team consider their purpose or goals of the play, their opponents' abilities, and their own strengths and weaknesses. Student writers need similar information. They, too, must have a repertoire of available strategies. They must be aware of their purpose for writing, predict obstacles that could be encountered while writing, and look inward at their own strengths and limitations with the process of writing. A football team must also evaluate the effectiveness of its strategies throughout the game. If game strategies are ineffective, new ones are selected that may be more appropriate. Similarly, student writers need to evaluate how well a writing strategy is working. If ineffective, they too must be willing to look for new and more successful ways to attain their writing goals.

The work of Harris and Graham (1992, 1996a), prominent researchers in the area of writing strategies who emphasize that the way in which strategies are taught is critical to their success, provided the background I needed to implement strategy instruction in Kate's writing workshop. Harris and Graham (1992) outline a few instructional features that are important to a successful strategic writing program:

- Strategies are best learned interactively.
- Strategy instruction makes invisible cognitive processes visible to students through dialogue.
- Strategies should be viewed as *temporary* supports to guide students' thinking.

These features are discussed in depth in the following three sections.

Strategies Are Best Learned Interactively

Strategic writing instruction is not simply a matter of *giving* students strategies to guide their writing processes. This type of instruction involves much more than the transmission of a strategy from expert teacher to passive student. Good strategy instruction calls for an interactive role between teacher and student. When strategies are learned interactively, learning becomes a shared responsibility. Success depends on engaging students as collaborators in their own learning.

Collins (1998) maintains that strategic writing instruction involves co-constructing strategies *with* students. The role of the teacher is to look closely into the difficulty a writer is experiencing and co-construct with the writer a strategic way around the difficulty. Freedman (1987) refers to this as "collaborative problem solving." Teachers in the writing classroom can work with students to co-construct strategies to fit students' specific struggles. In this way, strategy instruction becomes a collaborative effort between teacher and student. An important point to remember when using strategies to scaffold student learning is that strategies must be used as a support for the child within an interactive environment.

My ultimate goal with Kenda, Paulo, Daniel, and Amy was to create an interactive environment that provided the assistance that was necessary to move these young writers toward writing independence. Interaction through dialogue became an essential part of moving their writing growth forward. As Vygotsky (1934/1978) demonstrates, what students can do in cooperation with others leads to what they will be able to do individually in the future. The following exchange between Amy and me is an example of how our interaction brought detail and meaning to her writing:

Ms. C.:	Amy, the pocket watch is beautiful. What are you going to say about it in your piece?
Amy:	I don't know. I just don't know.
Ms. C.:	What does it look like? If I were the reader, I would want a detailed picture of the pocket watch in my mind. How might you describe this treasure in your writing?
Amy:	It is round.
Ms. C.:	Yes. What else?
Amy:	It is a little rusty.
Ms. C.:	Yes, it is. That is a good word. I like that. Can you include the word *rusty* in your paragraph?
Amy:	Yeah. Look! Only even numbers are on the front.
Ms. C.:	I didn't notice that.

| Amy: | It winds up and really works! Listen. [We listen to the tick, tick, tick...] |
| Ms. C.: | If you could carefully describe the features of the pocket watch in your writing, your readers might be able to see and hear it in their minds. |

Wells and Chang-Wells (1992) offer a theoretical perspective that presents talk as "the very essence of educational activity" (p. 26). Harris (1990) supports this perspective and further argues that collaborative dialogue between teacher and student should be recognized as a necessity for the developing writer. I found the role of dialogue to be critical to the teaching-learning process in the writing classroom. The ongoing interplay that occurred between teacher and learner provided the means by which support could be provided and adjusted.

In this classroom, our conversations were most successful when there was this collaborative effort between teacher and student. "The truly useful kind of talk is the dialogue of real conversation, the give-and-take interaction of two speakers, asking, answering, discussing, trying out, and exploring together, with neither monopolizing the conversation" (Harris, 1990, p. 151). Actively participating in the dialogue meant that both teacher and student were consciously attending to the conversation.

Amy:	This part about my great-grandfather...I don't have much to say.
Ms. C.:	What do you know about your great-grandfather?
Amy:	I know that he was old. He died a long time ago.
Ms. C.:	Where could you go to learn more about your great-grandfather?
Amy:	I can get more details from my mom...or else my grandma.
Ms. C.:	Amy, if you interview you mom and grandma you will be doing *research* for your piece.

This give-and-take element was important for students to take an active role in the construction of meaning. Bos and Anders (1990) write,

> The term "interactive" assumes that learning will be enhanced if the teacher and students utilize an interactive dialogue to discuss and organize concepts and to discuss and demonstrate strategic knowledge. This

interactive dialogue encourages cooperative knowledge sharing because the instruction calls for both the teacher and students to share their knowledge concerning content and strategies. Thus, the teacher serves as a mediator for learning. (p. 170)

Invisible Cognitive Processes Become Visible Through Dialogue

Graham and Harris (1989) remind us that mature writers conduct an inner dialogue that involves talking to themselves about their writing (see also Chapter 3). When encountering a complex writing situation, writers direct their thoughts by conversing with themselves. This personal dialogue instructs writers in how to solve the specific writing problems with which they are faced. Strategy instruction places emphasis on making invisible cognitive processes visible to students through dialogue (Englert & Raphael, 1989). (See Box 4.2 for additional resources on the role of dialogue in the writing classroom.)

Box 4.2
Resources on the Role of Dialogue in the Writing Classroom

Bruner, J. (1983). *Child's talk: Learning to use language*. New York: Norton.

Dyson, A.H. (1990). Talking up a writing community: The role of talk in learning to write. In S. Hynds & D.L. Rubin (Eds.), *Perspectives on talk and learning* (pp. 99–114). Urbana, IL: National Council of Teachers of English.

Englert, C.S., Raphael, T.E., & Anderson, L.M. (1992). Socially mediated instruction: Improving students' knowledge and talk about writing. *The Elementary School Journal, 92*(4), 412–449.

Englert, C.S., Raphael, T.E., Anderson, L.M., Anthony, H.M., & Stevens, D.D. (1991). Making strategies and self-talk visible: Writing instruction in regular and special education classrooms. *American Educational Research Journal, 28,* 337–372.

Geekie, P., & Raban, B. (1993). *Learning to read and write through classroom talk: Harwick papers on education policy*. London: Trentham Books Limited. (ED 365 414)

Gere, A.R. (1990). Talking in writing groups. In S. Hynds & D.L. Rubin (Eds.), *Perspectives on talk and learning* (pp. 115–128). Urbana, IL: National Council of Teachers of English.

Harris, M. (1990). Teacher/student talk: The collaborative conference. In S. Hynds & D.L. Rubin (Eds.), *Perspectives on talk and learning* (pp. 149–161). Urbana, IL: National Council of Teachers of English.

Manning, B.H., & Payne, B.D. (1996). *Self-talk for teachers and students*. Boston: Allyn & Bacon.

Palincsar, A.S. (1986). The role of dialogue in providing scaffolded instruction. *Educational Psychologist, 21,* 73–98.

Wilkinson, L.C. (1984). Peer group talk in elementary school. *Language Arts, 61*(2), 164–169.

Throughout this experience, I learned how to provide a means to represent the thoughts behind the writing process. I learned to put very specific words to the invisible writing process. For example, if I had been teaching these students about baseball, I would have provided a visual representation of how to swing the bat. If I had been teaching mathematics, I would have provided students with manipulatives such as blocks, beans, or popsicle sticks to explain the mathematical concept we were working on. With writing, however, I needed to use my language and conversation with the students to explain the cognitive aspects of this complicated activity.

I recall one day when Amy was trying to write an introduction to her piece. We were in the midst of a discussion on what makes a good introduction when I realized she did not know what an introduction was. "An introduction is a...it is a...a published thing!" she said. My response required careful reflection: How could I best describe an introduction to Amy? What were the features of an introduction that set it apart from the rest of a piece? Through dialogue, Amy and I came to a common understanding: An introduction can be found at the very beginning of any piece. It contains those first words that are to be read by the reader, so those words must be especially interesting because they need to capture the reader's attention. When a reader reads your introduction, you want him or her to think, "This sounds fascinating to me. I want to read more." I encouraged Amy to examine the opening sentences in published books. We learned that some writers begin a story with "Once upon a time...." Others begin by summarizing their entire story: "Every summer, I spend at least one week with my grandpa at our cabin." Still others begin by giving the reader only clues to the story ahead: "Mattie, a ballerina, loved to dance." With Amy, it became important to provide very clear, concrete direction and guidance, so that words accurately described the invisible thoughts behind crafting an introduction. Throughout, I was looking for language that was child-friendly. I pushed myself to find tangible ways to teach the hidden thoughts that support the writing process.

Vygotsky (1934/1978) tells us that this language for inner dialogue is acquired through interactions with others who are familiar with the process. Englert (1990) writes, "Teachers have an important responsibility to model writing strategies as they 'think aloud' to make visible the normally invisible cognitive processes related to planning, drafting, and revising text" (p. 215). When teachers think aloud in front of their students about their own cognitive writing processes, students hear the inner dialogue that mature writers use. This dialogue provides students with a framework that can guide and direct their own writing behavior. See, for instance, the following dialogue between me and Paulo:

Mrs. C.:	You don't know what to write about today, Paulo? When I can't decide what to write about, I try and think about all the things that are important or exciting to me and my life. Hmmm...I think about how I love to walk in a park near my house. I wonder...what parts of my walk could I write about? The colorful leaves in the fall? The slippery, frozen ground in the winter? The conversation I had with my friend as we walked? I wonder...can I describe what I see as I walk? What do you like to do, Paulo? What is important to your life?
Paulo:	Well, I really like sports. But, I have already written two sports stories.
Mrs. C.:	What kinds sports do you like?
Paulo:	All kinds of sports. I like basketball, baseball, football, even hockey. Hey! I haven't written one about snowboarding yet! [Paulo writes "Snowboarding" on his paper.] I have a lot to say about snowboarding.

Paulo continued to brainstorm other possible topic ideas. His mind became focused on winter topics, so he also wrote, "Snowball Fights" and "Making Snowmen." Paulo identified three possible topics and had a choice to make. Should he write about all three and title his piece "My Favorite Winter Activities" should he write a separate story for each activity? Paulo decided there was too much information for one story, so he wrote about his first choice, snowboarding.

Opportunities to think aloud can be provided to students as they practice the internal dialogue that occurs during writing. During interactions such as this one, it was important that Paulo took an active part in the dialogue. As time passed, Paulo began to take increasing responsibility for ownership of this inner speech when choosing a topic to write about.

*Reflection Point 4.1*_____

1. Many of us are not aware of what we do when we write. Think of a time when you wrote something you were really proud of. What process did you follow to write your piece? Where did you get your idea for this writing? What came easily to you? What was a struggle? How did you overcome your writing difficulties? How did you feel when your writing was successfully completed?

2. How can you bring your personal experiences with writing into the classroom? Write a description of this experience in your journal.

Strategies Provide *Temporary* Support

It is critical that teachers and students continually dialogue about the use of each strategy so students are aware of when to use the strategies and why they are important. It is equally important that teachers fade out the use of strategies as students become proficient with them. Strategies should be viewed as temporary supports to guide student thinking. Writes Englert (1990), "Strategy instruction is based on the assumption that the role of the teacher is to put themselves out of a job. In other words, good teachers help students become independent and strategic so that the teacher and support materials are no longer needed" (p. 216).

Strategic writing instruction teaches students to think carefully and strategically about their writing process. However, Harris and Graham (1992) contend that it should be viewed as only one small part of a student's development as a writer:

> Such development should occur in tandem with the development of a wide spectrum of writing and language skills, ranging from automatization of mechanics and skills involved in getting language onto paper, to the use of writing as a sophisticated means of expressing, exploring, and extending thought. (p. 149)

Thinking Strategically and Maintaining a Problem-Solving Focus

The term *strategy instruction* often calls to mind notions of traditional or transmissional forms of education. Strategies in the very traditional sense (imposed by the expert teacher; prescriptive; formulaic; a quick fix) do not fit into a process-approach/constructivist classroom. However, strategic writing instruction involves much more than *giving* students strategies to guide their writing process. Collins (1998) reminds us that strategic writing instruction includes a shift in thinking that encourages students to think strategically and maintain a problem-solving focus while writing. I believe mature writers think strategically when they write. Strategic thinking helps young students overcome the difficulties they experience in writing by encouraging a problem-solving focus. As teachers, our role is to help students identify specifically where it is they are experiencing difficulty and then work together in a "joint venture" to find ways to overcome students' writing difficulties. Teachers can help students learn to think strategically about writing by helping them co-construct strategies for themselves around their writing difficulties. When students assist in the development of personal writing strategies, they take greater control and ownership over their writing skills and writing processes. The strategies are most effective when they are understood and used by students in the midst of their difficulties. (See Box 4.3 for additional resources on writing strategies.)

Reflection Point 4.2

1. Audiotape some conversations you have with young writers in the midst of writing.

2. Listen to the tape and reflect on the dialogue that occurs. What kinds of conversations are you having with student writers? What questions are you asking to move their writing growth forward? How are you modeling the strategic aspects of writing instruction?

Box 4.3
Additional Resources on Writing Strategies

Collins, J.L. (1998). *Strategies for struggling writers*. New York: Guilford.

Collins, K.M., & Collins, J.L. (1996). Strategic instruction for struggling writers. *English Journal, 85*(6), 54–61.

Englert, C.S. (1990). Writing through strategy instruction. In T.E. Scruggs & B.Y.L. Wong (Eds.), *Intervention research in learning disabilities* (pp. 186–223). New York: Springer-Verlag.

Englert, C.S., & Raphael, T.E. (1989). Developing successful writers through cognitive strategy instruction. In J.E. Brophy (Ed.), *Advances in research on teaching* (Vol. 1, pp. 105–151). Greenwich, CT: JAI Press.

Harris, K.R., & Graham, S. (1992). *Helping young writers master the craft: Strategy instruction and self-regulation in the writing process*. Cambridge, MA: Brookline.

Harris, K.R., & Graham, S. (1996). *Making the writing process work: Strategies for composition and self-regulation*. Cambridge, MA: Brookline.

Pressley, M., & Woloshyn, V. (1995). *Cognitive strategy instruction that really improves children's academic performance*. Cambridge, MA: Brookline.

Chapter 5

Lessons Learned From Struggling Writers

Kenda, Paulo, Daniel, Amy, and I are becoming partners in the experience of learning to write. My presence alongside their desks no longer disturbs their work. The students just keep writing, stopping only to ask a question or explore their thoughts. I am enjoying the company of these four students. I have come to treasure our regular connections.

I arrived in the classroom one day to find Paulo working on his math assignment. His big brown eyes looked up and met mine. I winked. He winked back. I saw a smile on his face.

Kenda came instantly running up. "I read my story to Mr. Freeman today! He gave me four Werther's [candies]!" Mr. Freeman is the school principal, an important audience for Kenda's writing. After she shared her excitement with me, her hand reached in her pocket and pulled out one piece of Werther's candy. "You helped me, you know. This is for you," Kenda said softly.

Amy, beginning to rely on her own writing instincts, was working hard organizing her story on "Grandfather's Pocket Watch." After class, I complimented her on her hard work. "Amy, you should be very proud of this piece," I explained. In her excitement, her arms reached quickly around my neck for one brief hug.

Daniel, in the midst of frustration, came to me for help. His "Graveyard" story was suspenseful, but he didn't know how to get the main characters home safely after they found themselves locked in an upstairs bedroom. We discussed his many options. His confidence returned. The look in his eyes said, "I can do this now."

Just when I was beginning to think that writing growth was slow, that writing progress at times appeared to be at a standstill, these children re-energized me with the little things that made teaching so worthwhile. It was the small piece of candy, the wink, the hug, and that look of confidence. We are friends. In this experience, I have been reminded over and over that what really matters is the quality of interactions between teachers and students. No one approach matters more than teachers and students working together. When we work together we can learn so much from our students. With this information, we can place them at the center of our instruction and construct our teaching in response to their learning needs. We can gain insight into our students' knowledge, beliefs, and values.

Excerpt from Terri Christenson's journal
January 12, 1999

A primary goal of the Kids InSight series is to encourage teachers "to focus on individual students as persons and as learners—to keep kids in sight as we engage in teaching and learning practices" (Dillon, 2000, p. 151). Kenda, Paulo, Daniel, and Amy helped me gain insight into the struggling writers' perspective on writing instruction. Their learning in the writing classroom was shaped by their knowledge, beliefs, values, and previous experience as writers. The following questions emerged as the classroom teacher, Kate, and I tried to better meet the needs of these young writers:

- What can we learn from the struggling writer's perception of writing?

- How can we adjust our teaching to address the tensions experienced by struggling writers?

In this chapter, I will address these questions by sharing what Kate and I learned as we interacted with Kenda, Paulo, Daniel, and Amy. (See Box 5.1 for more questions to ask young writers.)

Perceptions of Writing

While I was getting to know each student I asked, "How did you learn to write?" Daniel and Amy responded:

Box 5.1
Questions to Glean Insights From Young Writers

As teachers, we commonly ask questions to evaluate student response. In contrast, I encourage you to ask the following questions not to evaluate but to discover what young writers know, believe, and value about writing.

- Do you like writing? Why or why not?
- How did you learn to write? Who helped you?
- Do you consider yourself to be a good writer? Why or why not?
- What does a good writer need to know in order to write well?
- What things do you do well in writing?
- What do you find easy about writing?
- Have you ever written something you have been especially proud of? What made your piece so good?
- What difficulties or problems do you have as a writer?
- When you get stuck trying to express an idea in writing, what do you do?
- What would you like to learn next in order to become a better writer?
- Did you write much last year? If yes, what did you write? How has your writing changed in the last year?
- What does your teacher do to help someone who is having trouble writing? Would you do it differently if you were the teacher?
- Do you ever write when you are at home? What kinds of things do you write at home?
- How do you decide which are your best pieces?
- How do you go about choosing topics to write about?
- How do you decide what ideas to include in your writing?
- How do you revise your writing?
- What do you do when you come to a word you don't know how to spell in writing?
- Where can you write the best? When do you write the best?
- Would you like to be an author someday?

Daniel:	Uhhh...I was watching my parents and my brothers. They were the ones that taught me to print.
Amy:	My Grade 1 teacher...she gave us all a little booklet and she helped us print and all that. It was a booklet that taught me how to write letters. Like *e* and *E*.

I could see their interpretations of how they learned to write focused on printing and handwriting rather than composition. As a result, I asked

Amy, "Was there any teacher who helped you create stories?" She responded, "No. I can't remember anybody. They taught me mostly handwriting, like in Grade 3. She'd give us a handwriting book. Then she'd show us how to write a big capital *A* and a little *a*."

My interaction with Paulo resulted in this conversation:

Ms. C.:	What kinds of things about writing did you learn?
Paulo:	I think handwriting and printing.
Ms. C.:	Did you create stories?
Paulo:	I don't remember.

Kenda carried on a lengthy conversation describing the details of her writing journey, in which teachers also emphasized handwriting rather than composition. She even provided a written visual aid for me.

| Ms. C.: | How did you learn to write Kenda? |
| Kenda: | In kindergarten we would have to write *A A A A A A A*. In Grade 1, we would not have the lines and she would get us to write like this: *Cat dog Appol*. In Grade 2, we would write longer sentences, like this: *I wint campin in the woods with my dad and mom*. We made sentences in Grade 2. In Grade 3, we'd write *AAA*, only in [cursive] handwriting: *AAA BBB CCC DDD*. In Grade 4, we would write sentences in handwriting: *I wint campin in the woods with my mom and Dad*. |

Kenda's, Paulo's, Daniel's, and Amy's responses support research done by Graham, Schwartz, et al. (1993), who found that struggling writers often hold a narrow view of what writing involves. For struggling students, learning "to write" often means being able to print and handwrite. As noted in Chapter 2, Kenda held the narrow view that her writing was at its best when every letter was formed correctly and her paper looked extremely neat:

Ms. C.:	Kenda, will you open up your workshop binder and show me your very best writing?
Kenda:	That is it. Right here....
Ms. C.:	What makes this piece so good?
Kenda:	I wrote neatly.

I found that these beliefs about writing influenced what and how struggling writers went about composing. For Kenda, success with writing meant her papers needed to be written neatly. As an observer, I could see this was a high priority in Kenda's writing process. She started each first draft on a fresh piece of paper and concentrated intently on her penmanship. It was important that each letter was formed exactly as she had been taught in her handwriting lessons. It became clear that this emphasis on neatness interfered with her ability to focus on the meaning of the piece.

For Kenda's writing growth to move forward, she needed a broader perspective on writing. I wanted her to see that mature writers do not complete neatly written first drafts. To demonstrate this, I brought in the book *Hooray for Diffendoofer Day!*, by Dr. Seuss, Jack Prelutsky, and Lane Smith (1998). The back of this book provided visual examples of the rough drafts created by the authors to produce this written story. With this example, we could visually see how Dr. Seuss changed and rearranged his thoughts. For example, sometimes it became necessary for him to cross out or take away sections of his writing, whereas other times it became necessary for him to add new ideas to his work. The result was a messy rough draft with a lot of great ideas. I wanted Kenda to understand that there need not be fear about making mistakes while writing. Authors understand that writing can be changed or transformed easily.

One day following this demonstration, I tucked Kenda's eraser back into her pencil box and encouraged her to cross out and draw lines through the words or phrases she did not like in a particular piece of writing. To reassure Kenda, I showed her my field notes filled with crossed-out words, rewritten phrases, and insertions and said, "This is the way a rough draft can look." From our discussions, Kenda began to learn that the process of writing could be messy. It was not a neat and orderly process that produced a perfect first draft. In addition, Kenda could begin to see that the focus of a writer's thoughts should initially be on idea generation. It became important for her to realize that writing involved much more than creating a neatly handwritten piece. (See Chapter 3 for more discussion of strategies used with Kenda.)

It is possible that this narrow view of writing stems from writing instruction that once reflected a traditional orientation. I am a product of this traditional form of writing instruction. As a student, I remember that teachers chose my writing topics for me. Often I did not know much about these topics, nor did I have an interest in writing about them. When I was asked to produce a written draft, I turned in my first draft as my final copy. Many students' narrow views of writing most likely reflect this traditional form of writing instruction.

Ideas behind the teaching of writing have changed dramatically since my schooling experience. Writing process theory has influenced what we know about how children learn to write, and as a result, our role as teachers in the writing classroom has changed. We now see writing as a process to be experienced, not a product to be evaluated. We encourage our young writers to take the time needed to generate ideas and make plans and to explore what to say and how to say it. We want young writers to understand that good writing often reflects good rereading and rewriting of a piece.

Although educators have made great strides toward implementing this process approach to writing instruction, many teachers still tend to favor the more traditional approach. We may value what the research is saying, but when time becomes tight and our energies become low, we often return to the way we were taught. With backgrounds of experience in traditional classrooms, teachers can find it difficult to focus on new ways of thinking about writing instruction.

Reflection Point 5.1 _____

1. How has the role of writing teacher changed over the past 25 years?

2. What qualities make an effective writing teacher today? Share your thoughts with a colleague and seek his or her thoughts on this topic.

_____

With the historical perspective of writing instruction in mind, my work with these four students focused on developing their understanding of writing as a process. It was my hope that they would begin to understand the key concepts behind process theory. Kate and I reinforced six concepts in her classroom:

1. Mature writers do not complete perfect first drafts.

2. Writing often must be shaped and reshaped, written and rewritten to achieve a desired end result.

3. Sometimes it is necessary to add or take away sections of writing before completing a written piece.

4. New ideas continually emerge while writing.

5. There need not be fear about making mistakes while writing. Authors understand that writing can be easily changed or transformed.

6. Writing takes time. Pieces we are proud of are generally not written quickly.

Reflection Point 5.2

1. Begin to glean insight from the thoughts of your students by informally interviewing them as they write (see Box 5.1 on page 92 for sample questions). How do the students in your classroom view writing? What are their perceptions of writing instruction? Record and carefully analyze their responses to questions such as, What makes a good writer? Craft other questions that will allow you to uncover students' beliefs on writing.

2. Reflect on how their thoughts may influence their writing process.

3. How will these insights have an impact on your teaching?

4. Write a summary of the interview experience in your journal.

Tensions Experienced by Struggling Writers

Ms. C.: What do you do when you are writing and you come to a word you don't know how to spell? What do you do?

Kenda:	I look in the dictionary, and if I can't find it in the dictionary, I'll ask you. If you are not around, I'll ask the teacher. Usually...sometimes I'll ask Jocelyn, but sometimes she won't respond. So, sometimes I'll ask you, sometimes I'll ask the teacher, and sometimes I'll just look harder. Sometimes I get REALLY STRESSED OUT! AHHHH!

I watched these four writers experience many of the frustrations and obstacles that come with learning to write. Learning to write well is not easy for anyone, but for struggling writers, there are more opportunities for annoyance and irritation. Struggling writers often have a low tolerance for difficult or problematic situations. Frustrations surface quickly and easily. Each time they are faced with a writing obstacle, frustrating feelings can interfere with their ability to problem solve their way out of the difficulty. (See Chapter 2 for discussion of some of these frustrations.)

The struggling writers with whom I interacted often were sent subtle messages from others in the classroom that their writing did not measure up or their ability was lacking. With these messages came the uneasy feelings that cause self-doubt to surface. I found the emotions of all four students to be tied to a very weak sense of self-efficacy. At the edge of every conversation sat questions such as, Am I doing this right? Is this wrong? Am I a bad writer? This isn't very good, is it? These questions were not always verbalized but were apparent in the looks on their faces and in their tentative body language.

Paulo provides a perfect example. He entered class each day after recess as a happy, energetic, and involved boy. As soon as writing workshop began, the sparkle in his brown eyes began to fade. He began to doubt his worth and his behavior reflected disinterest. Paulo did not want to write. This led to resistance, which protected him from his emotions and helped him maintain a sense of confidence. In other words, if he did not participate, he did not have to deal with his feelings of inadequacy. Deep within, he was protecting himself the only way he knew. While Paulo was resisting writing, however, other students in the class were becoming fluent with it.

Kenda also experienced feelings of inadequacy. She spoke freely with me about her feelings:

| Ms. C.: | What is the hardest part about writing for you? |
| Kenda: | Getting it done.... Sometimes, I'm a little too slow. Sometimes I just sit and sometimes I spell a lot of things wrong, and it is really embarrassing when someone has to check it. 'Cuz when Jennifer was checking it, she was saying every word that I got wrong out loud, and I felt really bad. Look—this is what Jennifer wrote: "Great story. Spelling is quite bad." |

Kenda was sensitive to peer opinion, and frustrations surfaced when she needed to share her work with others. She became tense whenever it was time for a peer to provide feedback on her writing. This self-consciousness limited her access to useful help from peers. Kenda wanted to feel good about sharing her writing, but there were many days when she just could not. There were too many difficult previous experiences to overcome.

Because Kate and I sensed these difficulties, changes were made in the classroom routine for Kenda. When it was time for a peer confer-ence, Kenda came to me first. We reviewed her writing, focusing on the many positive aspects of the piece. We also shared the responsibility for editing. In this way, Kenda could approach her peers with confidence. She knew the strengths of her piece and was comfortable knowing that she had carefully attended to the many details she often found frustrating. From working with these students, I learned that how writers cope with frustration and feelings of inadequacy can be critical to the success of their writing experiences.

Reflection Point 5.3

Initiate a discussion with a fellow writing teacher. Ask the follow-ing questions:

1. How do you establish a positive tone for writing in your classroom?

2. How do you assist students in dealing with the frustrations of writing?

Recognizing Student Achievement and Building Writing Confidence

Recognizing the writing achievements of all four struggling writers and building their writing confidence became a priority of our instruction. When I first stood at the side of Kate's classroom watching her students write, the students experiencing difficulty with writing were not hard to find. Kenda was fiddling in her desk, focusing on any distraction that came her way. Paulo sat far back in his chair, arms crossed, gazing around the room. The most serious aspect of Daniel's writing was the appearance of his paper. There were numerous misspellings. And Amy, having difficulty settling in on an interesting topic, connected her writing problems to a lack of worthwhile ideas and experiences. These classroom behaviors provided an outward expression of the difficulties these students were experiencing.

As stated throughout this book, my main goal in working with these students was simple: I wanted to convince them that they had the ability to write. Often, they were overwhelmed by all that they *could not* do. Believing in the abilities of each student encourages students to build on their successes. When writing is going well and children are enjoying the process, their energy for writing increases.

Sadly, such encouragement is more easily talked about than done. When struggling writers display resistant or defiant behaviors, it is difficult to build their writing confidence. When I first began working with Paulo, it was hard work. He was an uncooperative and unwilling participant. It was easier for me to move to working with another writer, one that welcomed my presence. Paulo's resistance to writing instruction required more energy on my part than I often had, but returning to his desk on a regular basis demonstrated interest in his writing.

The experience with all four students affirmed for me something I have always believed—all children, even struggling writers, can grow as writers. Some students require more scaffolding than others, but all can make writing progress. A key ingredient in their growth is a learning environment that supports their natural enthusiasm for writing. The writing progress of these young writers was due largely to an increased self-confidence, which grew out of the positive responses of everyone with whom they shared their work. When the thoughts and feelings expressed in their writing were received with enthusiasm, Kenda, Paulo, Daniel, and Amy began to discover themselves as writers. As Dyson (1990) comments,

> In the end, then, our most important teaching tool may not be any one teaching strategy or instructional material. Rather, it may well be the sort of stance toward children that we adopt. The most helpful stance would seem to include an appreciation of children, not simply as budding writers, but more important, as interesting people with experiences, opinions, and ideas to share with us and, just as important, with each other. (p. 113)

I have learned that recognizing struggling writers' accomplishments—no matter how small these growth steps are—promotes positive self-concepts and increases self-confidence.

Peer Conferences

Robeck and Wallace (1990) found that students develop a self-concept based largely on how they compare themselves to others, including siblings, classmates, and significant adults. This has implications for the struggling writer in the midst of a peer conference. During this research, I found that peer conferences could be a time of discomfort for the struggling writer.

I often asked myself, however, What were these struggling writers learning from peer conferences? I could see that peer conferences served a host of functions. Conferences bring groups of students together to explore the process of writing. Regular conferences with peers give students a chance to talk about their writing. Conferences with friends help to create a writing community (Smith, 1988). When writing communities are established, support systems are put into place, and students have a place to turn with their specific questions. This classroom dialogue acts as a scaffold, guiding writers toward new learning. Peers provide an authentic audience for student writing (Wilkinson, 1984). In addition, as students share their thoughts and insights with one another, they become more familiar with their own writing processes and gain broader perspectives on the nature of writing (Gere, 1990). Strong writing instruction cannot depend only on the dialogue that occurs between teacher and student. Dyson (1990) writes, "A strong system cannot depend only on talk between teacher and child. The social energy that is generated among the children themselves—their own desires for individual expression and social communication—may infuse writing itself" (p. 112).

Vygotsky (1934/1978) contended that thought and language develop through social interactions. He asserts that thinking must proceed from the group to the individual, and inner speech (the language used for thought) develops when children shift collaborative forms of learning to the realm of inner personal functions (see Box 5.2 for more resources on Vygotsky's theory of language and learning). In the writing classroom, then, the ability to solve writing problems is often possible because students have the chance to engage in exploratory talk with other peers. Ideas can be developed, problems can be solved, and new ideas can be made possible through the use of language. Englert and Mariage (1991) also remind us of the important role those peer conferences can play in writing development. These researchers write, "It is chiefly through dialogue among students that the writing processes are internalized and owned by students" (p. 341).

During peer conferences, struggling writing *are* learning many things about writing and responding, but they also are learning some lessons that are not as easy to address. For instance, during peer conferences struggling writers can be reminded—sometimes over and over—that their writing is less than it should be. They have to deal with the uneasiness of bringing forth underdeveloped writing. As struggling writers hear and read the writing of more talented writers, they question their own pieces. Further, these regular peer interactions often open the sensitive writer to criticism from insensitive peers, which can shatter egos and confidence, thus impeding writing growth. Peer conferences can bring fear, feelings of inadequacy, and weakness to the surface. Lensmire (1994a), a teacher researcher, followed the peer relationships of young writers in a third-grade classroom. He too became aware of the powerful role social context was playing in workshop settings. The assumption that all writers were being supported by these peer-oriented experiences was not accurate. Consider, for example, the following vignette from Kate's classroom:

Box 5.2
Resources on Vygotsky's Theory of Language and Learning

Dixon-Krauss, L. (1996). *Vygotsky in the classroom: Mediated literacy instruction and assessment.* White Plains, NY: Longman.

Everson, B.J. (1991). Vygotsky and the teaching of writing. *The Quarterly of the National Writing Project and the Center for the Study of Writing and Literacy, 13*(3), 8–11.

Goodman, Y.M., & Goodman, K.S. (1990). Vygotsky in a whole-language perspective. In L.E. Moll (Ed.), *Vygotsky and education: Instructional implications and applications of sociohistorical psychology* (pp. 223–250). New York: Cambridge University Press.

Vygotsky, L.S. (1978). *Mind in society: The development of higher psychological processes* (M. Cole, V. John-Steiner, S. Scribner, & E. Souberman, Eds. & Trans.). Cambridge, MA: Harvard University Press. (Original work published 1934)

One day, Brent was peer editing Daniel's baseball story. As the boys settled on the floor in the back of the room, there was the initial chatter that occurs when friends gather, but the boys soon got right to business. Brent took his job of peer editing quite seriously, and Daniel was happy to begin this next stage of his writing process. Brent read quietly and then crossed out word after word. I could see the discouraged look on Daniel's face as the minutes passed. Brent took a deep breath and said, "Wow. This is gonna take me all day." It did. The boys returned to their desks when the writing period was over. Daniel held up his marked paper in his hand. "No one will read this," he muttered quietly to me.

Within the environment of collaborative learning, struggling writers can experience shyness, anxiety, intimidation, and feelings of inadequacy. How does a teacher make these issues explicit to a classroom filled with peers? How do we negotiate solutions when we are dealing with such sensitive issues? What kinds of intervention should teachers provide? Establishing a safe environment for writing is key to answering the previous questions. Calkins (1994) writes, "We cannot write well if we are afraid to put ourselves on the page. We cannot write well if we are afraid to let our individual voice stand out from other voices" (p. 143).

We teachers can provide support to young writers by structuring classroom time to model the techniques of effective writing conferences.

We can include minilessons during our writing periods that address the following questions: What qualities make a good writing conference? How can we best talk to our friends about their writing? What is the responsibility of a peer in a writing conference? What does it feel like to receive criticism on our writing? How can we promote positive attitudes toward writing through our comments? How can we best reinforce the writing efforts of our friends? Guidelines for peer dialogue can be modeled by role-playing specific conference situations. Share with your students the list of guidelines for effective peer conferences in Box 5.3. In the words of Calkins (1994),"Children are likely to be respectful and supportive of each other when we mentor this kind of behavior and when our classrooms are warm, safe communities" (p. 143).

We can also model an effective peer writing conference during our own writing conferences with students. McIver and Wolf (1999) attribute the mature dialogue that can occur in peer conferences to the instructional techniques used by the classroom teacher: "Peer conferences provide the opportunity for students to engage in the same activities that characterize teacher/student conferences.... These peer conferences, however, are dependent on the skillful model the teacher presents" (p. 56). What we say to students and how we say it provides a powerful model for their

---

Box 5.3
Guidelines for an Effective Peer Conference

1. Encourage the writer to read his or her work out loud.
2. The listener can respond by asking questions such as
   - What are you trying to say here?
   - Can you tell me more about...?
   - What parts of your writing are you most pleased with?
   - Where have you experienced the most difficulty?
   - What specific help would you like from me?
3. Together, the writer and listener should identify those things the writer has done really well.
4. Conclude by identifying one way the writer can make his or her piece more interesting.

interactions. When we carefully choose our responses to young writers, we are modeling a way of responding to other writers. Our methods of interacting with student writers can set a tone for response in the classroom.

However, despite all our good intentions and attempts at creating a warm, welcoming writing environment, there will still be writers in our classrooms who evade peer interaction to avoid uncomfortable feelings.

Ms. C.:	Do you conduct peer conferences, Kenda?
Kenda:	A lot of people ask me, but I don't want to.
Ms. C.:	Why not?
Kenda:	I'd rather not do them. I don't know. If they spelled a word right and I, by accident, checked it off wrong...I wouldn't like that.

Teachers can help young writers like Kenda find the confidence they need to share their writing by reminding them that "writing is so often about making mistakes and feeling lost" (Lamott, 1994, p. 163). *All* writers experience feelings of insecurity or intimidation when they expose their writing to others. Lamott (1994) recognizes some of the emotions that can surface when our writing is shared:

> I know what a painful feeling it is when you've been working on something forever, and it feels done, and you give your story to someone you hope will validate this and that person tells you it still needs more work...it may strike you as a small miracle that you have someone...who will tell you the truth and help you stay on the straight and narrow, or find your way back to it if you are lost. (pp. 163–164)

Express to students that ultimately we can learn a great deal from a reader's honest feedback. The difficulties involved in exposing our writing to others can offer great pleasure and personal satisfaction when we view our writing from another's perspective. Although poorly constructed criticism can impede writing development, there is a need for constructive criticism that can help young writers grow. I have learned that what is required for all writers is a response that balances honest feedback with encouragement and praise.

*Reflection Point 5.4*_____

1. Observe student writers as they interact in a peer conference. Write an account of the interaction. Reveal the thoughts and emotions of each student involved, and reflect on these questions: What were these writers learning from the interaction? What were they thinking? What were they feeling?

2. What can we learn from students' interactions?

_____

Sensitive and Encouraging Response

Ms. C.:	Paulo, have you ever written something you are really proud of?
Paulo:	Well, yes.... One was "The Kid Who Became an Elf" because all the teachers liked it, and you brought it to your kids and you said they liked it.

How adults respond to young writers has a powerful impact on how the students view themselves as writers. In the brief preceding conversation, Paulo had decided that this story was good, not because of the effort he put into it or the quality of the piece, but because everyone else liked it. For Paulo, "The Kid Who Became an Elf" was a turning point in his attitude toward writing. When other writers responded to his story with positive remarks, Paulo found the motivation to write more.

The affective and emotional dimensions of learning influence how students will respond during their writing period. According to Dwyer and Dwyer (1994), "Odden (1987) reported agreement among researchers that when teachers demonstrate positive attitudes toward their students as capable learners, their students will, in fact, perform more successfully" (p. 68). Good and Brophy (1987) also found teacher attitudes toward students to be a critical factor in influencing student achievement. Cleary (1991) also makes a good point:

> If our job as writing teachers is to teach students a skill that they may use after graduation, then it's ironic if the major role we play is as purveyor of criticism. We may teach the skill, but we kill the students' desire to use it in the future, making the act of teaching futile. (p. 51)

Feelings of confidence emerge when young writers are reminded of their strengths and recognized for their accomplishments.

My most significant and enjoyable contribution to the four students with whom I worked was building confidence in their ideas and abilities. Encouragement and positive constructive feedback were required regularly for each writer. Kenda, Paulo, Daniel, and Amy began every writing period with little memory of their successes or their prior day's accomplishments, as if their chalkboard of confidence had been erased at the end of each day. Every time we worked together, their blank confidence chalkboard needed to be filled with positive reminders that strengthened their motivation. These students thrived on small forms of recognition from me, such as smiles, pats, and winks. An example of this confidence follows:

Ms. C.:	What made that story so good?
Kenda:	Hmmm...the little bit more help that I'm getting.
Ms. C.:	You are getting some help on that story...
Kenda:	[interrupting]...A LOT of help!
Ms. C.:	Do you know what, Kenda? You are getting help, but that story is *yours*. *You* came up with the idea, and *you* wrote it. That story is good because of *you*, not because of anybody that helped you. That story is good because you worked hard on it.

Teacher expectations also can play a major role in students' achievements. If we believe these students can become more thoughtful, reflective writers, then they will. Christophel (1990) concludes that if students come to the classroom unmotivated, teachers can help students use their communicative behaviors to improve their motivation levels. Motivation to write surfaces when writers feel like they are active and contributing members of the writing classroom. Their motivation to learn is directly tied to their engagement with writing, and what they believe about their capabilities affects their writing progress. Despite their writing difficulties, these students really do want to feel competent and good about what they write. Closely tied to their difficulties is a desire to perform at higher levels. Because each of these four students wanted to be good writers and wanted their writing to be respected, recognizing and appreciating their efforts played an important role in increasing their motivation to write.

We cannot expect children to work out the complex feelings of inadequacy themselves. It requires assistance from adults and other children in their surroundings. Nonthreatening instructional situations allow students to develop their potential and can motivate them while doing so. I have learned that for children to accept the challenge of going beyond their current writing ability, they must feel accepted and safe. (See Box 5.4 for resources about the affective and emotional dimensions of learning.)

Reflection Point 5.5

1. Collect several writing samples from the students in your classroom and carefully analyze each piece.

2. What steps can you take to view student writing from a growth perspective? As you examine individual writing samples, ask yourself the following questions:

   • What does this student know about writing?

   • What is this student doing really well?

   • What are the writing achievements of this piece?

3. Choose one piece on which to focus, and identify the abilities of the young writer. Then look for ways to move his or her growth forward. Ask yourself,

   • What positive comments can begin instruction?

   • What is one way I can develop this student's writing?

> **Box 5.4**
> **Further Resources**
> **on the Affective and Emotional Dimensions of Learning**
>
> Christophel, D.M. (1990). The relationship among teacher immediacy behaviors, student motivation, and learning. *Communication Education, 39*, 323–340.
>
> Dwyer, E.J., & Dwyer, E.E. (1994). How teacher attitudes influence reading achievement. In E.H. Cramer & M. Castle (Eds.), *Fostering the love of reading: The affective domain in reading education* (pp. 66–73). Newark, DE: International Reading Association.
>
> Graham, S., Schwartz, S., & MacArthur, C.A. (1993). Knowledge of writing and the composing process, attitude toward writing, and self-efficacy for students with and without learning disabilities. *Journal of Learning Disabilities, 26*(4), 237–249.
>
> Heathington, B.S. (1994). Affect versus skills: Choices for teachers. In E.H. Cramer & M. Castle (Eds.), *Fostering the love of reading: The affective domain in reading education* (pp. 199–208). Newark, DE: International Reading Association.
>
> Pintrich, P.R., & Schunk, D.H. (1996). *Motivation in education: Theory, research, and applications*. Englewood Cliffs, NJ: Merrill.

Teaching Responsively

The time I spent in Kate's classroom encouraged me to think more about my teaching practices and reflect on how teachers respond to students in the writing classroom. The most satisfying aspect of this experience was the change that occurred in me. Throughout this experience, I was learning alongside the students. With each passing day, as I became more aware of my own actions, I began to monitor critically my own behavior and refine my abilities as a reflective practitioner. Throughout, I learned about what it means to be a teacher of writing. Supporting the struggling writer required the ability to teach responsively.

I must admit, there were times that I worried: Did my ways of interacting with students resemble my old ways of teaching? Whenever I said the word *strategy*, I was reminded of traditional strategy instruction—imposed by the teacher, prescriptive, and formulaic. It did not fit what I was doing in this process approach classroom. Although my interactions with these students often looked like miniature lectures, they were really very different because I was *teaching responsively* within the context of each student's writing. First, these students engaged in their own work of creating stories. Then, I tried to identify, suggest, or demonstrate what might help them the most. Teaching responsively, within the context of each student's writing, meant instruction could be tailored to meet the needs of individual writers. Students could be met within their personal zone of proximal development and led toward writing growth (Collins, 1998).

Writers of all ages—especially struggling writers—need partnerships with more experienced mentors. We mature writers, teaching responsively, can provide student writers with insight and guidance in understanding writing and the writing process. When mature writers model or scaffold problem solving for young writers, we focus student attention on specific aspects of their writing difficulty. Eventually, students are able to internalize the problem-solving process and attend to their writing difficulties without prompting or guidance.

Teachers can use writing conferences as one way to provide the modeling needed for effective writing. The teacher-student conference is an ideal place for teachers to address specific writing needs. Individual students can meet with a teacher at any stage in their writing process. They can bring forward their questions and writing issues important to them at the time. In this way, teachers can address the writing needs of individual students and co-construct personally meaningful strategies to help individuals grow as writers.

When our writing classes are filled with 25 or more students, it can be difficult to teach to the writing needs of individual writers. When our classes are large and we are not able to spend time with individual writers each day, then we need to find other ways to help students progress. There are many ways for teachers to address this. We can first gather our students in large or small groups to explore writing issues. At the start of each writing period, we can use minilessons as a place to introduce specific writing strategies or address specific learning needs. We can put our own writing on an overhead projector and show our students how we address our writing dilemmas, or we can build on the work of our students and create minilessons from their writing needs. This planned instructional time brings a sense of community to a writing workshop and addresses the needs of many students at one time.

We also can invite other adults into our classroom who are interested in helping students with the writing process. For example, volunteers can provide a wonderful ear for the beginning writer. They can pull their chair alongside student desks and listen to students read their pieces.

Volunteers can ask questions, respond to questions, and motivate young writers. Additional school personnel can also be invited into the classroom during workshop time. Kate welcomed a teacher's assistant and learning assistance teacher into her classroom to help writers throughout the writing workshop period. We can tap into the resources that surround us for additional teaching support.

We can also employ the strengths of our students for support in the writing classroom. Suppose you have a student who is a whiz with a thesaurus and enjoys finding "just the right word." When a writer cannot think of the word he or she wants to use, this student expert can be turned to for brainstorming help. Or, suppose you have a student who enjoys conversing with peers when they do not know what to write about next. This student can become a resource to other writers who want to rely on exploratory talk for identifying meaningful topics. Perhaps you have a student who has learned to identify paragraphs in writing. Others writers could turn to him or her for help when questions on paragraph structure arise.

In the writing classroom, young writers can benefit from their conversations with other writers. John-Steiner (1985) refers to this kind of interaction as an "apprenticeship":

> Learning by being with a knowledgeable partner is a more effective method of developing a particular language of thought than learning from books, classes, or science shows. The crucial aspect of these informal or formal apprenticeships is that they provide the beginner with insights into both the overt activities of human productivity and into the more hidden inner processes of thought. (p. 200)

Smith (1988) also describes the social and collaborative nature of literacy learning. He, too, believes that students learn more when they work in an environment of collaboration with mentors. Harste (1990) further summarizes this view: "Language is a social event. Most of what we know about language has been learned from being in the presence of others" (p. 317). Teachers and peers who guide writing development become an important part of the classroom environment because they are knowledgeable about writing concepts and writing strategies important to growth. Support from other writers can help students move from one level of learning to a higher one as they gain mastery of a given task. Writes Dixon-Krauss (1996), "Children gradually come to know and understand the content knowledge that others in their environment know and understand" (p. 79).

The process of learning through interaction with others has been described by Vygotsky (1934/1978) as taking place within the zone of proximal development. Vygotsky's zone of proximal development describes "the distance between the actual developmental level as determined by independent problem solving and the level of potential development as determined through problem solving under adult guidance or in collaboration with more capable peers" (Vygotsky, 1934/1978, p. 86). Vygotsky argues that instruction aimed at the actual developmental level is ineffective, because it is aimed at behaviors that the child has already mastered. Similarly, aiming instruction far beyond the proximal level is equally ineffective. Our goal, as teachers then, is to aim toward instructional activities that fit within the zone of proximal development. Learning generally occurs as students work within their zone of proximal development and connect current knowledge and skills to new knowledge and skills.

My role as a teacher in the writing classroom was to find and then work within each student's zone of proximal development. Through conversation and questioning, I tried to find each writer's current level of understanding and help to move their thoughts into their next "zone," therefore extending student thinking. These interactions with students required that we both come to the learning task as partners and active participants. Students brought their interests and learning needs to the task, whereas I brought content and specific strategies that may be helpful to their writing development. Together, we negotiated their learning goals.

To effectively teach responsively also required that I develop in-depth *teacher knowledge of writing and the writing curriculum*. Understanding writing enabled me to generate a variety of strategies or prompts to stimulate student thinking in appropriate directions. This kind of responsive teaching also required *knowledge about learners' abilities and interests*. This became especially important because students were not always able to communicate the specific aspect of their writing difficulty. In order to scaffold effectively, I needed an in-depth understanding of their abilities, needs, and interests. Teaching responsively also required that I develop *knowledge of myself as a writer*. I found myself regularly turning inward and reflecting on my own writing processes and the strategies I use for overcoming a writing difficulty.

Knowledge of the Writing Curriculum

Teachers need specific knowledge to teach writing effectively (Scheid, 1991). Each day in the writing classroom, teachers serve as writing models, explicitly illustrating to students the procedures, thinking, and inner dialogue that occurs while writing. This demonstration requires an awareness of the writing process and how problems encountered in writing may be addressed.

For me, this meant reflecting on the writing process and strategies of effective writers. Prior to beginning my classroom research, it was necessary for me to gain an understanding of the various instructional approaches to teaching writing, including process writing (Atwell, 1987; Calkins, 1994; Graves, 1983); self-instructional strategy development (Harris & Graham, 1992, 1996a); cognitive strategy instruction (Englert, 1990); and strategic writing instruction (Collins, 1998). This provided the framework I needed to talk to students about their writing and helped me to reflect on my own writing process so I could verbalize to students strategies I had once acquired intuitively.

This background knowledge was critical to teaching responsively. I was able to bring this background knowledge into our conversations every day. A broad understanding of the field of writing also gave me the confidence to follow my intuitive impulses as I responded to student struggles.

Knowledge About Learners' Abilities and Interests

As I learned to personalize my writing instruction, I found the assessment of individual writers' strengths and weaknesses to be at the heart of responsive teaching. Collins (1998) encourages teachers to become familiar with the current writing strategies of struggling writers, so we can use them as starting points to begin our instruction. Becoming familiar with individual student needs and current strategies required detailed observation and a careful analysis of student behavior and interactions. From these observations, I identified specific areas of difficulty and tried to focus on those dilemmas. For example, from observing Paulo's writing process, I knew he would benefit from a discussion on topic selection. I began looking for ways to help him think about what it was he was doing, rather than focus on the frustrations.

How did I know Amy would benefit from planning and organizing her writing? From observing her as she wrote, I could see Amy lacked a vision in her writing. I began looking for ways to help her think about developing her ideas and putting them into a logical order before writing. Personalizing instruction—whether it be with individual students, small groups, or the entire class—becomes a part of responsive teaching. In the writing classroom, this requires a focus on the needs of students, rather than on specific instructional content.

Knowledge of Oneself as a Writer

Each day I spent in the writing classroom, I found myself thinking reflectively about my own writing process. What did I do when I could not settle in on a topic? What did I do when I got stuck writing and did not know what to say next? What did I do when my piece was ready for revision? How did I feel when my writing was exposed for others to read? I became intimately familiar with my writing process as I spent time with these children. My experiences as a writer were at the heart of our interactions. To teach writing well requires first-hand experience with the dilemmas that accompany writing. Responsive teaching requires knowledge of myself as a writer.

Bringing my own writing experiences into the classroom allowed me to see how important it is for teachers to write with their students. Smith (1988) says so much of learning is being around people who do it well. Power and Ohanian (1999) write, "Imagine taking pottery lessons from someone who has never handled clay, or photography lessons from someone who's never touched a camera. It's not necessarily critical that teachers write well, but they do need to try to write well" (p. 250).

*Reflection Point 5.6*_____

A writing notebook provides opportunities for a writer to collect and assemble ideas for writing before setting out to write. Fletcher's book, *Breathing In, Breathing Out: Keeping a Writer's Notebook* (1996), offers suggestions and many ideas for keeping a writing notebook. Fletcher writes,

> Keeping a notebook is the single best way I know to survive as a writer. It encourages you to pay attention to your world, inside and out. It serves as a container to keep together all the seeds you gather until you're ready to plant them. It gives you a quiet place to catch your breath and begin to write. (p. 1)

1. Begin your own writing notebook. Write about the thunderstorm you experienced last evening, the new friend you met, watching your daughter's basketball game, your reaction to a movie, or an interesting conversation you experienced.

2. Bring your notebook into your classroom and read excerpts to your students. Provide a model for students from which they can begin to create their own writing notebooks.

3. Use students' writing notebooks as a place to begin writing instruction.

Although great strides are being made by educators toward understanding the teaching and learning of writing, "many teachers themselves do not value writing as an activity, nor do they enjoy writing" (Scheid, 1991, p. 41), but when teachers write with their students they demonstrate the value of writing. Emig (1971) writes, "teachers of composition should themselves write in both the reflexive and the extensive mode so that when they teach, they are more likely to extend a wider range of writing invitations to their students" (p. 4). Graves (1991) refers to these teaching examples as "learning stories" (p. 144). We can say to children, "This is what I learned and this is how I learned it." As we share the thinking behind our own writing process, we model the strategies we use for over-coming difficulty.

During this particular classroom experience, my field notes provided an opportunity for sharing my writing process. The students were always curious about what and why I was writing in that messy notebook. By sharing my notes, I was able to demonstrate many writing behaviors:

- My notebook was a place for "capturing" my thoughts.
- It was a place where I could quickly write down my ideas, without worrying about spelling or handwriting.
- My notebook helped me to "pay attention" to the activities around me.
- It was a place to keep all my thoughts together.
- From these notes, my writing could begin.

My field notes demonstrated for students the messy part of writing. My disorderly pen marks written across the page became a model for the students' rough drafts. My students could see the lines crossing out words, the arrows, and the added thoughts. My notebook was real, something they could touch and see.

Struggling writers face many challenges as they experience the writing process. This chapter explored their perceptions of writing instruction and reflected on some of the conditions necessary for writing growth to occur. Before reading the next chapter, take time to address the questions in Reflection Point 5.7.

Reflection Point 5.7 _____

1. Based on your knowledge of writing instruction, make a list of the most important qualities of an effective writing program.

2. How will you bring these qualities into your experiences with children?

Chapter 6

New Directions in Teaching Struggling Writers

I like [writing] now 'cuz I've got this long story, "I Turned Into a Dinosaur," and I've got lots of ideas, and I can think of ideas and...it is fun writing your own stories because they might even go into your own book.

Paulo

S truggling writers need a special kind of help. These students need to learn to value themselves as writers and as learners. They need to find a feeling of competence and link this with the motivation to write. Struggling writers have amazing thoughts, but because of repeated cycles of failure, they need help learning to appreciate and value their ideas. When they set aside the notion that they are incapable, their motivation for writing increases. This attitude change encourages the very experiences that help them to become better writers.

Englert and Mariage (1991) write, "As more experienced members of a larger community of writers, teachers play a primary role in apprenticing students into the inherently social functions of writing" (p. 330). In other words, the teacher in the writing classroom can play a critical role in helping students move toward writing independence. Our knowledge, our abilities, and our attitudes can influence the lives of struggling writers and scaffold student writing growth.

Signs of Growth

As teachers scaffold student growth, we always are watching for signs of progress. The signs of writing growth that appeared in Kate's classroom were not always easily apparent. I must admit, there were days when I did not think I saw any writing development. Student work seemed to plateau. My minilessons were occasionally met with students' blank stares and wandering thoughts. Writing was a slow and difficult process for these students. It often took weeks for particular students to work through the entire writing process and complete one piece. But then, just when I thought growth was at a standstill, small signs of progress began to emerge from Kenda, Paulo, Daniel, and Amy.

Kenda, for example, wrote seven or eight lines by herself one day. That *real* story she wanted to write was near completion. She had written three chapters. Feeling confident and looking for affirmation, Kenda cautiously asked her friend Jennifer to read her work. She said, "Do you like my writing? I could change it if you don't." I thought about how difficult it must be to share writing with a peer when lacking confidence, yet Kenda was gaining confidence and becoming brave. She was initiating conversation about her writing. This was growth.

Kenda's writing fluency was also slowly increasing. She worked best when I moved my chair alongside her desk. "What are you up to today?" I would ask. This prompt helped to refocus her writing energies. She made great strides in her work when I simply sat next to her. Fewer and fewer mistakes were made while Kenda copied her final draft. She even put a notebook under her bed at home to catch her ideas.

Paulo, who previously closed his binder during the middle of writing workshop as a sign of disinterest, began spending more than a few minutes developing a piece. Paulo was no longer wandering around the room or fiddling at his desk. He was writing. For the first time, he began to work at developing a piece, a story about a Christmas elf (see Figure 14).

Paulo's ideas for this piece quickly fell into place. He started with a small idea and watched it grow on paper. This was a turning point for Paulo and his writing. The teacher loved it, the kids loved it, and Paulo was proud. "I thought this was going to be another boring story like I always

---

Figure 14
Paulo's Story

The Kid Who Became an Elf

One day a little boy name Derek Elf was going to school. Everybody made fun of him because of his last name. He said he didn't care, but he did. He wanted to leave the city. So he did. He said he would go to the North Pole because nobody would find him. He packed his bags and left.

It took him a while to get there, but he didn't care. Then he saw a toy factory. He ran there and knocked on the door. A little elf answered the door and the elf let him in. Derek couldn't believe his eyes. There were toys everywhere and in front of him was Santa! Derek said, "Hi!" When Santa saw him, he made him an elf. It would be fun working with Santa and his elves. Santa gave him a special gift. It was an elf suit. It was green and it fit perfect. Now he would not be laughed at again because of his last name.

---

write," he confessed. Because he was pleased and proud of reactions to his work, he began to view himself as a writer.

Daniel, whose writing was typically one long piece, began initiating his own questions about putting paragraphs into his stories. He had observed others indenting and he wanted to know more about how to include indents in his own writing. While working on his story about go-carts, Daniel circled groups of ideas in his writing. These circles formed the foundation of a paragraph structure for his final draft (see Appendix C for more on this Boxing Strategy). Daniel was demonstrating writing progress by grouping ideas together and forming paragraphs in his writing (see Figure 15).

Amy began to generate ideas on her own, working especially hard during the stage of prewriting. Tremendous growth was apparent, especially in the formation of her ideas. Amy arrived at school one day carrying a treasured pocket watch that had belonged to her great-grandfather. A story about this family heirloom had been mulling around in her thoughts for many days. I could see that Amy cherished this watch by the way she held it, touched it, and looked at it. The watch also came carefully wrapped in three layers of Kleenex, all folded neatly. Every few moments Amy would polish the surface of this antique. Her peers were curious.

Figure 15
Daniel's Story

Go-Carts

I like go-carts. Go-carts are small cars. They have small wheels. They all have different colours. There are no doors or windows. Some of them have numbers. The front is low, and the back is high. The engine is in the back. The engine is like a lawn mower because you have to pull the chord to start it. Go-carts are made of plastic and steel.

You ride them at a go-cart place. There should be a special track. There should be some turns. There should be wheels for the wall because if you smack the wall, the wheels will protect the go-cart. Did you know about a cart that has an orange flag? That tells you a child is in the go-cart.

It feels amazing to ride a go-cart. It feels like you're riding a small car. If you step on the brake the go-cart stops quickly. If you press the gas, it goes forward and you can't go backwards.

Have you ever ridden a go-cart before? I have ridden ones before. I am going for my birthday. It was really scary. I had to go by myself the first time. It was scary when someone hit me with their go-cart. My heart beat really fast because I was nervous.

As Amy began her story, the pocket watch rested at the edge of her desk. She carefully examined its details while trying to write a description of the watch:

> I wondered what it looked like when it was new. The inside has a second hand. The hands are rusty. The hands move, but it does not tell the right time. The even numbers are on the watch and the odd numbers are little squares. The squares sparkle. It looks like it has little stars...The minutes are marked by little lines. The numbers you can't see because they are faded away...I turned the time winder and it started to work!

Memories of her great-grandmother and great-grandfather surfaced as she wrote, also. Amy was learning to take the fine details of her life and make them meaningful. To an outsider, her great-grandfather's watch was just an old, dirty, broken watch; to Amy it was a family treasure that carried a history of life experience and connected Amy to her heritage. She had begun to realize that her life was worth writing about. (See Figure 16 for a sample of Amy's story.)

The writing sample in Figure 16 shows that Amy was beginning to write with awareness and curiosity. Her piece became filled with descriptive

> ### Figure 16
> ### Amy's Story
>
> My great grandma was born in 1900. Her birthday was in February. She was 12 years old when Titanic sank. She lived in Norway. She gave us lots of hugs. She always squeezed me. When she got older she moved in a nursing home. We would go for walks and I pushed her wheelchair.
>
> She died this last summer. My grandma cried and all my aunties and uncles cried too and my family cried. When she died she was 98 and she was as old as the year, 1998.
>
> My great grandpa was born in 1905 in Minnesota. He married my Grandma Arneson in 1926. They farmed in Tuffnell. They had ten kids. He loved kids. He always was good to everyone.
>
> He was good natured. He died in 1960 at age 54. He died before I was born.
>
> This pocket watch is special to me because it helps me remember my great grandparents. I am taking good care of the pocket watch. I have a special place to keep it.

words and emotion. I did not know if this descriptive writing would stay with her the next week, but I learned that one special story can make a difference. This was a turning point in Amy's writing. She was writing with renewed confidence. Amy began researching her ideas, interviewing her mother and grandmother about a great-grandfather she never knew. Amy learned to cherish the stories behind the pocket watch. I learned to cherish the stories behind the children.

Reflection Point 6.1

1. Examine the writing portfolios of the students in your classroom. Carefully tune into their abilities and write a description of growth that has been occurring.

2. Analyze students' writing, asking yourself, What are the subtle indicators of writing growth? How do I know students are moving ahead in writing development?

Strategy Instruction and the Process Approach

Teachers, spurred by the process movement, are changing the nature of writing instruction in our schools. The benefits of implementing process writing are many (Atwell, 1987; Calkins, 1994; Graves, 1983; Murray, 1996), but despite the potential advantages of process writing, the approach has generated some concerns among teachers (Lensmire, 1994a, 1994b; Spiegel, 1992). Process writing has been viewed as being based on indirect rather than direct methods of instruction (Graham & Harris, 1994). A notion exists that writing workshops prohibit the scaffolded development of strategies and skills. As a result, some teachers are concerned that the process approach may not provide enough support for students who face challenges in learning to write (Mather, 1992).

The debate over how to teach writing to students who experience difficulty with the process continues. The field is divided between those who teach writing as a sequence of specific skills and those whose teach writing based on a process approach. I have come to understand that we can do both. Teachers implementing the process approach can integrate instruction and model for writers a variety of effective writing strategies. We may incorporate the spirit and theoretical orientation of the process movement while we provide explicit and focused explanation for helping students become independent writers. We can provide the best of both worlds for our students.

Many teachers have come to believe that there is something wrong with explicit teaching (Graham & Harris, 1994). They value discovery learning in the writing classroom and work hard to provide opportunities for students to untangle the complex writing process themselves. Strategy instruction has been criticized for not placing enough emphasis on the learner's active construction of knowledge (Borkowski, 1992; Poplin, 1988). I must, however, ask, Is learning to write natural? Is this a process that children can discover themselves? Vygotsky (1934/1978) would respond by saying that learning to write requires interaction with more knowledgeable members of the culture. Because writing is so difficult and complex, it becomes important for teachers to provide the instructional scaffolding necessary for young writers to untangle this complex process (Vygotsky, 1934/1978). Rogoff and Gardner (1984) agree, adding, "Effective instruction may require the teacher to lead the learner through the process, with both involved in the activity" (p. 101).

Instead of seeing process writing and strategy instruction as conflicting positions, I believe we can consider integrating them in a complementary fashion. Within the context of authentic student writing, we can present the skills and strategies needed for writing growth to occur (Collins, 1998; Harris & Graham, 1996a; MacArthur, Schwartz, et al., 1991; Spiegel, 1992). Through individual conferences or group minilessons, we can teach specific procedures, skills, and strategies in response to students' needs. We can provide support for individuals, small groups, or the entire class to help them learn the craft of writing. Students can then apply what they have learned to their own writing pieces.

There is so much we can teach about the writing process and learning to write, but when the conditions are right there are also many things students can teach themselves and each other. We can allow for both kinds of learning to occur in the writing classroom (Collins, 1998). We can build bridges between strategy instruction and the process approach to address the needs of our struggling writers.

The inquiry in which I engaged with four young learners in one classroom demonstrated to me that the workshop environment can be a powerful context to develop strategies and skills. I found that although the process approach works well with all writers, it seems to be particularly successful with struggling writers. Within a workshop environment, teachers and students can share the responsibility for solving writing difficulties. In this way, teachers can be collaborative participants, helping writers move toward new learning. Specifically, I learned that the writing process approach can

- encourage writing experiences to be tailored to fit the needs of individual writers (Cason, 1991);

- allow for strategies to be taught within the context of the students' own writing (Collins, 1998);

- encourage the interactive element necessary for students to take an active role in their writing growth (Bos & Anders, 1990); and

• emphasize a problem-solving focus, helping students to think strategically about their own writing by reflecting on the process (Flower, 1981).

For students like Kenda, Paulo, Daniel, and Amy, who experienced difficulty identifying and developing specific writing strategies, more extensive, explicit instruction was also required. This help meant integrating strategy instruction into their writing workshop. Write Harris and Graham (1996b), "In successful integrated instruction...teachers conduct ongoing assessments of each student's abilities, skills, knowledge, motivation, social characteristics, and prior experiences. They then arrange whatever support children need—from direct explanation through discovery" (p. 27).

Teaching with a process approach does not mean that we should abandon explicit instruction. As teachers, we are responsible for providing demonstrations in lessons and conferences. We can share our knowledge as we collaborate with students in the process of learning to write.

Reflection Point 6.2

Recently, there has been an increased interest in balanced literacy instruction. In your journal, address the following questions:

1. How would you define balanced writing instruction?

2. Why is this an important topic?

3. What influences may be attributed to this trend?

Recommendations for Further Research

My inquiry project with Kenda, Paulo, Daniel, and Amy has moved me toward new understandings; however, many questions remain about how to best meet the needs of struggling writers in an elementary classroom. Some suggestions for further study include the following:

- This study shares the experiences of four students in one fifth-grade classroom. It would be advantageous to investigate other student experiences from different schools and different age groups. How are the experiences of the young writers in this study similar to or different from the experiences of struggling writers at different schools or age groups?

- I left these four learners wondering how their writing will progress in the future. Graves (1983) suggests that students need time to grow in their writing ability. An obvious extension of this research would be to pursue a longitudinal study of struggling writers. What are the experiences of struggling writers who spend several years in process-approach classrooms?

- For the students in my study, proofreading was a long and laborious task. Incorrect spelling also restricted their ability to communicate effectively. I could see that computers might have the capacity to ease some of the difficulties that struggling writers experience. It might be interesting to investigate how word processing might help or hinder these writers.

- My investigation focused on struggling writers; however, each day in the classroom I observed the tentative interactions that surfaced between the four struggling writers and their peers. I am curious how teachers might best facilitate collaboration between struggling writers and other writers in the classroom. What conditions are necessary for successful and productive collaboration? Throughout this experience, peer conferences often opened up the sensitive writer for criticism. It became obvious that these conferences occasionally placed struggling writers into uncomfortable situations. I am also interested in finding out how peer conferences might be modified to better support the needs of the struggling writer.

- I could easily see that the journey toward writing independence might not be an easy road for the struggling writer. Atwell (1987) reminds us that growth in writing is slow. Growth can be so slow that we often do not see progress until we put two pieces written by the same student side by side. This slow growth is especially true for the struggling writer. In this study, I had to look very carefully for signs of student progress. The small growth that occurred could have easily gone unnoticed. I am interested in finding out how teachers can more accurately observe and measure the quiet progress of struggling writers. What are the specific and subtle indicators of writing growth?

*Reflection Point 6.3*_____

Review your responses to the Reflection Points in this book.

1. What insights have you gained about struggling writers?

2. What have you learned about the teaching of writing?

3. How will you incorporate these new discoveries into your classroom?

4. Predict some of the tensions you may encounter as an elementary school teacher of writing. Write a summary of your thinking.

Looking Back

I had two primary goals for writing this book. First, I wanted to share the experiences of struggling writers in a process-approach classroom. Second, I wanted to demonstrate how teachers can model strategic thinking for their young student writers. In Chapter 1, I provided an overview of the experience by briefly introducing you to the students, the teacher, and the classroom setting. Chapter 1 also provided an opportunity for me to position myself within the context of this study. Chapter 2 looked closely at the abilities and specific frustrations of struggling writers. Chapter 3 presented some of the interactions that took place between me and the four student writers in Kate's classroom. Chapter 4 presented suggestions for building writing strategies, and in Chapter 5, I reflected on the insights I gained from working with struggling writers.

My interpretation of my findings from working with four struggling writers supports integrating skill and strategy instruction into process-approach classrooms (Collins, 1998; Graham & Harris, 1994; Mather, 1992; Spiegel, 1992). These components of instruction are essential for these learners. The basic assumption underlying this perspective is that struggling writers can be taught more effective strategies for dealing with writing dilemmas than the strategies they apply informally on their own. Thinking strategically in the writing classroom helps students develop their skills as writers by teaching them new and different ways of thinking about the process.

My personal experiences as I sought to understand these young people allowed me to reflect and learn from the children. I have gained a more in-depth understanding of how to "read" the writing classroom. When I wrote about my experiences in this fifth-grade classroom, I paid more attention to what was going on around me. For the first few days in the classroom, I walked through the rows of desks not really seeing much. The room was crowded in my head—Paulo needed his pencil sharpened, Kenda's glue had leaked in her desk, and Amy's socks were uncomfortably wet from the snow. All these things prevented me from "being present." I had to walk through the rows of desks several times before I began to tune into the children and their writing. Once I did, I started noticing that Kenda smiled when I pulled my chair alongside her desk, Amy preferred to spread out her writing on the big table, and Paulo sent a strong message by using his shoulder as a fortress between him and me. It was difficult to read the classroom when I was preoccupied with other things, but when I wrote my field notes, my lens became clear. My experiences became sharper, and I saw things that otherwise might have been missed. I was learning how to listen and observe the details of teacher-student and student-student interactions.

During the months spent in this fifth-grade classroom, I learned to make sense of the little things that took place in a familiar environment. It was the little things that my memory most easily recalls: the familiar sights and sounds of the classroom, the smell of the school when the children entered after recess, the look on the faces of interested and concerned parents, the touch of paper crumbled in frustration, and the images of four young people who welcomed me into their writing journey.

For me, this has been a journey of tremendous value. It has helped me understand the prominent role writing should play in any classroom. The reason the teaching of writing is important to struggling students is that they do far more than learn to write. Students learn to make choices and carry out decisions, identify and solve problems, and view themselves as active and contributing members of a community. I have experienced a journey that has invited me to become an advocate for making the necessary changes important for the success of struggling writers. Reflections from my final journal entry sum up what I learned from this experience:

> My eyes now scan the familiar classroom. At each desk, young writers are working. Some work together. Some work alone. These children have truly become a community of writers. As I look at each student's face, memories of the past 5 months surface. I smile at the sight of Kenda, her dark hair, brown eyes and pretty smile. She is proud to show me another page in her fashion design book.
>
> There is Paulo. He brought his writing journal back to school to show me the lengthy story he wrote at home. Paulo displays his work with such pride. There is Daniel, still working on his graveyard story. I wonder what finally happened to those characters. Did they escape alive? And there is Amy. She has just written a good-bye note for me in her new writing journal.
>
> Improving each student's writing ability and writing confidence was at the heart of this experience, but so much more was gained. We became friends. The names and faces of these students will leave lasting impressions on me, not just because they provided me with valuable information about writing and how it is learned, but also because we connected.
>
> I have shared the experience with them.
>
> I have shared in their writing journey.

Cognitive Strategy Instruction in Writing (CSIW)

nglert, Raphael, Anderson, Anthony, and Stevens (1991) developed a series of writing strategies called Cognitive Strategy
Instruction in Writing (CSIW). The strategies are solidly grounded in current theories of the process-writing approach, and have been
designed to guide students and teachers through the stages of planning,
organizing, drafting, editing, and revising. The mnemonic "P.O.W.E.R."
stands for plan, organize, write, edit, and revise. "Think-sheets" have been
devised that correspond to each specific writing subprocess. These sheets
guide students through the entire writing process by focusing on the
metacognitive processes in writing. They provide students with an opportunity to observe the writing process that guides mature writers. (Adapta-
tions of these think-sheets begin on page 131.)

CSIW, based on verbal modeling, or think-alouds, explicitly provides
students with the "hows" of writing. Specifically, teachers model and think
aloud their thoughts as they write. The think-sheets provide a framework for teacher-student dialogue about writing and serve as prompts
for student thinking. Students are interactively involved in dialogue to
internalize and reinforce the writing strategies presented.

The think-sheets are the most visible component of CSIW. However,
they do not stand alone. The think-sheets are merely one small part of a
writing curriculum that emphasizes writing as a process. It is critical that
teachers and students continually dialogue about the use of each strategy
so students are aware of when to use the strategies and why they are

important. It is equally important that teachers fade out the use of think-sheets as students become proficient with the writing strategies. Think-sheets should be viewed as temporary supports to guide student thinking. As students become confident with the process of writing, dependency on the think-sheet is reduced.

Planning Think-Sheet

Name:_____ Date: _____

Topic:_____

Who: Who am I writing for?

_____

_____

Why: Why am I writing this?

_____

_____

_____

What: What do I know? (Brainstorm)

1._____

2._____

3._____

4._____

5._____

6._____

7._____

8._____

How: How can I group my ideas?

_____

_____

_____

Adapted from C.S. Englert, T.E. Raphael, L.M. Anderson, H.M. Anthony, & D.D. Stevens, as cited in Pressley, M., & Woloshyn, V. (1995). _Cognitive strategy instruction that really improves children's academic performance_. Cambridge, MA: Brookline, p. 159.

Organizing Think-Sheet

Name:_____ Date: _____

Topic:_____

Explanations

What is being explained?

_____

_____

In what order do things happen?

First,_____

Second,_____

Third,_____

Fourth,_____

Finally,_____

Clues: Who does it? What things do you need? How do you do it?

_____

_____

_____

_____

Adapted from C.S. Englert, T.E. Raphael, L.M. Anderson, H.M. Anthony, & D.D. Stevens, as cited in Pressley, M., & Woloshyn, V. (1995). *Cognitive strategy instruction that really improves children's academic performance.* Cambridge, MA: Brookline, p. 160.

Self-Editing Think-Sheet

Name:_____ Date: _____

Topic:_____

Read. Reread my paper.

What do I like best? (Put a * by the parts I like best.)

What parts are not clear? (Put a ? by unclear parts.)

Question Yourself. Did I...

Tell what was being explained?	Yes	Sort Of	No
Tell what things you need?	Yes	Sort Of	No
Make the steps clear?	Yes	Sort Of	No
Use key words?	Yes	Sort Of	No
Make it interesting?	Yes	Sort Of	No

Plan. Look back.

What parts do I want to change?

1._____

2._____

Write two or more questions for my editor.

1._____

2._____

3._____

Talk. Talk to your editor.

Read your paper with your editor. Then the editor should read the paper and complete the Peer Editor Think-Sheet. Next, meet and talk about your answers.

Adapted from C.S. Englert, T.E. Raphael, L.M. Anderson, H.M. Anthony, & D.D. Stevens, as cited in Pressley, M., & Woloshyn, V. (1995). *Cognitive strategy instruction that really improves children's academic performance*. Cambridge, MA: Brookline, p. 161.

Peer Editor Think-Sheet

Name:_____ Date: _____

Read. Read the paper.

What is the paper about?

_____

_____

What do you like best? (Put a * by the parts you like best.)

What parts are not clear? (Put a ? by unclear parts.)

Questions yourself. Did the author...

Tell what was being explained?	Yes	Sort Of	No
Tell what things you need?	Yes	Sort Of	No
Make the steps clear?	Yes	Sort Of	No
Make it interesting?	Yes	Sort Of	No

Plan. Look back.

What two parts would you change?

1._____

2._____

One thing that would make it more interesting is

_____

_____

Talk. Meet and talk with the author about his or her paper.

1. Compare your comments.

2. Talk about how to fix up the paper. Help the author if he or she wants

   help.

Adapted from C.S. Englert, T.E. Raphael, L.M. Anderson, H.M. Anthony, & D.D. Stevens, as cited in Pressley, M., & Woloshyn, V. (1995). *Cognitive strategy instruction that really improves children's academic performance.* Cambridge, MA: Brookline, p. 162.

Revising Think-Sheet

Name:_____ Date: _____

1. What suggestions did your editor give? Put a check next to the
   suggestions you will use.

   a._____

   b._____

   c._____

   d._____

2. How will you make your paper more interesting?

   _____

   _____

3. Go back to your first paper and make your revisions.

REVISION SYMBOLS

Type of Revision	Symbol	Example
Add words	∧	The girl is my ∧ sister. *(little)*
Take out words	—	The woman ~~has~~ tried
Change order	∽	to give. He had go to home.
Add ideas here	⌐	The dog is friendly. *(Tell which dog.)*

Adapted from C.S. Englert, T.E. Raphael, L.M. Anderson, H.M. Anthony, & D.D. Stevens, as cited in Pressley, M., & Woloshyn, V. (1995). *Cognitive strategy instruction that really improves children's academic performance*. Cambridge, MA: Brookline, p. 163.

Appendix B

Strategies for Composition and Self-Regulation

Strategy instruction is also the focal point of a writing program for young writers developed by Harris and Graham (1992). These researchers address a wide range of cognitive writing strategies designed to make the writing process more clear to young writers. They address specific strategies for text structure, as Englert and colleagues have done in Cognitive Strategy Instruction in Writing (CSIW), but they extend their focus to include strategies for goal setting, self-instruction, self-monitoring, and self-reinforcement. These strategies are intended to assist struggling writers in self-regulation and independently managing the writing process.

Writing Process Strategies

Basic Three-Step Strategy

This basic writing strategy can help guide the planning and writing process. (See Harris & Graham, 1996a, p. 75.)

1. *Think*—Who will read this? Why am I writing this?

2. *Plan* what to say.

3. *Write* and say more.

Story Grammar Strategy

Harris and Graham's (1996a) story grammar strategy is remembered most easily by its visual form:

W-W-W

What = 2

How = 2

Once a writer calls the mnemonic to mind, further thoughts or questions based on the mnemonic are recalled that can guide writing:

<u>W</u>ho is the main character; who else is in the story?

<u>W</u>hen does the story take place?

<u>W</u>here does the story take place?

<u>What</u> does the main character do; what do other characters do?

<u>What</u> happens when the main character does or tries to do it? What happens with the other characters?

<u>How</u> does the story end?

<u>How</u> does the main character feel; how do the other characters feel?

Brainstorming—A Planning Strategy

Brainstorming can help students generate content for their pieces. (See Harris & Graham, 1996a.)

Think of a good story idea.

Write down good words for my story.

Write my story—use good words and make sure my story makes sense.

Read back over my story and ask myself—did I write a good story?

Fix my story—can I use more good words?

SPACE—A Planning Strategy

With this strategy, the mnemonic SPACE is used to assist students in recalling the key prompts. (See Harris & Graham, 1996a.)

Note <u>S</u>etting.

Note <u>P</u>urpose.

Note <u>A</u>ction.

Note Conclusion.

Note Emotions.

Report Writing Strategy

This strategy will assist students as they write reports for content area subjects. (See Harris & Graham, 1996a.)

Brainstorm what you want to know and what you want to learn.

Organize your information on a web.

Gather new information and revise your web.

Use the web as you write.

Keep planning as you write.

Check the web: Did you write what you wanted to?

SCAN—A Revising Strategy

This strategy reminds student writers of the important role revision plays in the writing process. (See Harris & Graham, 1996a.)

Read the first draft of your essay.

Find the sentence that tells what you believe. Is it clear?

Add two more reasons why you believe it.

SCAN each sentence

- Does it make SENSE?
- Is it CONNECTED to my belief?
- Can I ADD more?
- NOTE errors.

Make my changes on the computer.

Peer Revising Strategy

This strategy gives support to peers as they provide important feedback to their classmates' writing. (See Harris & Graham, 1996a.)

1. Revise
   - Listen to the writer and read along.
   - Tell what the paper is about and what you liked best.
   - Read and make notes. Is everything clear? Can any details be added?
   - Discuss your suggestions with the author.

2. Proofread
   - Check your paper and correct errors.
   - Exchange papers and check for errors in

     Sentences—Read each sentence. Is it complete?

     Capitals—Are first letters of each sentence capitalized? Are proper nouns capitalized?

     Punctuation—Is there punctuation at the end of every sentence?

     Spelling—Circle words you are not sure of. Check spelling with your word list, spelling checker, or dictionary.

   - Discuss corrections.

The Six Basic Types of Self-Instructions

Writers use self-talk to regulate their writing behavior. These self-instructions are aimed at helping writers guide and monitor their writing task. (See Harris & Graham, 1996a.)

Problem Definition

Size up the nature and demands of the task:

- What is my purpose?
- What is it I have to do here?
- What is my first step?

Focusing of Attention and Planning

Focus on the task at hand and generate a plan:

- I have to concentrate, be careful, think of the steps.

- To do this right I have to make a plan.

- First, I need to...then...

Strategy

Engage and implement writing or self-regulating strategies:

- First I will write down my essay writing reminder.

- The first step in writing an essay is...

- My goals for this essay are...

Self-Evaluating and Error Correcting

Evaluate performance; catch and correct errors:

- Have I used all my story parts? Let me check.

- Oops, I missed one; that's OK, I can revise.

- Am I following my plan?

Coping and Self-Control

Subsume difficulties or failures and deal with forms of anxiety:

- Don't worry; worry doesn't help.

- It's OK to feel a little anxious; a little anxiety can help.

- I'm not going to get mad; getting mad makes me do poorly.

- I can handle this.

- I need to go slowly and take my time.

Self-Reinforcement

Provide rewards:

- I'm getting better at this.

- I like this ending.

- Wait 'til my teacher reads this!

- Hurray—I'm done!

Self-Monitoring

As writers compose, they monitor their progress and self-assess both their writing process and written products. This act of self-assessment can be made visible to writers through dialogue and the following basic checklists. (See Harris & Graham, 1996a.)

Time and Place

_____I set up a schedule for when I would work on the paper.

_____I found a quiet place to work.

_____I got started working right away.

_____I kept track of how much time I spent working on this paper.

_____I always had the materials ready that I needed each time.

_____I sat down to work.

Understanding the Task

_____I read or listened to the teacher's directions carefully.

_____I asked the teacher to explain any part of the assignment that was unclear to me.

_____I restated what I was supposed to do in my own words.

Planning

_____I thought about who would read my paper.

_____I thought about what I wanted my paper to accomplish.

_____I started planning my paper before I actually started writing it.

_____I used a strategy to help me plan my paper.

Seeking and Organizing Information

_____I tried to remember everything I already knew about this topic before starting to write.

_____I got all the information I needed before starting to write.

_____I organized all the information I had gathered before starting to write.

Writing

_____I thought about what I wanted my paper to accomplish as I wrote.

_____I thought about the reader as I wrote.

_____I continued to develop my plans as I wrote.

_____I made revisions in my paper as I wrote.

Revising

_____I revised the first draft of my paper.

_____I checked to make sure that the reader would understand everything I had to say.

_____I checked to make sure that my goals for the paper were accomplished.

_____I made my paper better by adding, dropping, changing, or rearranging parts of my paper.

_____I corrected errors of spelling, capitalization, punctuation, and the like.

_____I reread my paper before turning it in.

Seeking Assistance

_____I asked other students for help when I needed it.

_____I asked my teacher for help when I needed it.

_____I asked my parents or other people for help when I needed it.

Motivation

_____I told myself I was doing a good job while I was working on the paper.

_____I rewarded myself when I finished the paper.

Appendix C

Strategic Writing Instruction

Collins (1998) presents a balanced approach to writing instruction by integrating skills and process in what he calls Strategic Writing Instruction. This balanced approach encourages the systematic teaching of strategies within a process-approach classroom and allows for the gradual, scaffolded transfer of responsibility from teachers to student writers. Collins encourages teachers to "think strategically about writing and the teaching of writing so that they can help writers identify and use strategies to control their own writing skills and writing process" (p. viii).

Collins (1998) argues that struggling writers in the classroom are not deficient in writing ability. Rather, he suggests, they prefer strategies that are often suppressed in schools. He encourages teachers to become familiar with the current writing strategies of struggling writers, so we can use them as starting points to help students begin to think strategically about their writing. Collins uses the term *default strategies* to describe a "group of frequently occurring, developmentally recursive strategies writers may resort to when a writing task becomes sufficiently challenging" (p. 113).

I like to think of the default strategies writers fall back on as being similar to my default meals I often prepare in the evening at home. When life becomes challenging, I make sure there are two default meals readily available in my cupboard: spaghetti and tacos. I resort to one of these two meals when the task of preparing a meal seems overwhelming. My culinary skills extend beyond these two meals, but I always revert back to them when the going gets tough around 5:00 p.m. I do not discard, nor does my family discourage, the use of these default meals. New and creative dinner menus are frequently attempted and presented, but they do not replace my dependable spaghetti and tacos.

Similarly, struggling writers fall back on default strategies when writing tasks seem overwhelming. The three default strategies characteristic of struggling writers include copying, visualizing, and narrating (Collins, 1998). Collins points out that these are strategies many of us automatically turn to when faced with daunting writing tasks because these strategies are familiar and reliable.

As teachers, we do not have to discourage the use of these strategies to make room for new ones. Rather, the new strategies learned can be connected meaningfully to default strategies. Writers add to their list of successful strategies as they gain experience with the writing process, but they do not give up existing strategies as they acquire and learn new ones. Collins encourages teachers to look for opportunities to build on the default strategies of student writers.

Copying

Copying is a prevalent strategy used by struggling writers when the writing gets difficult. I recall many students who have copied the work of someone else and tried to make it their own. From these experiences, copying has received negative connotations; many educators refer to copying as cheating. Collins looks at copying from a different perspective, though, and argues that some forms of copying can be learning and planning strategies that are helpful in promoting writing development.

Copying strategies are commonplace in the growth and development of most learners. As my own two children learned to talk, their vocabulary was acquired by mimicking or copying the words of others. When the phone rang, my daughter would pick up her toy telephone and mimic my voice with a friendly "hello." My son learned to write his name by copying the letters I had written at the top of his artwork. We do not have to look far to see children learning by copying.

Copying can help writers in many ways. I have watched young writers borrow the thoughts and ideas from a book they are reading. From these sources, they can acquire language and rhythms of writing new to their writing repertoire. Professional writers even use a copying strategy by borrowing the thoughts and ideas of other authors as they synthesize and report current research. Says Collins, "There is nothing wrong with the copying strategy when it is used to conceive but not to deceive" (p. 144). Instead of telling students not to copy, educators should help writers learn ways to transform copied materials to support their own ideas. Collins presents the following strategies that can be used to build on a writer's natural tendency to imitate.

"I Wish I Could Write Like That" Strategy

This strategy reminds me of my days as a preschool teacher. Many mornings on my way to work I would compose a song to a familiar tune. The structure of the music was already in place, and I simply would insert my own words and thoughts into the established rhythm. In a writing classroom, students can put their own words into a professional writer's text structure (Collins, 1998). Collins is not encouraging plagiarism. The basic rule for imitating others' writing is, "Keep the form, but change the words and the meaning" (p. 148). In the example in Figure 17, a student writer reworked "If I Were in Charge of the World," a poem by Judith Viorst (1981), by changing the words and the meaning, but keeping the form.

Exposing struggling writers to the writing style of published authors can expand the variety of these students' writing. From these published pieces, student authors can emulate writing style, structure, and word choice. We can learn many things by imitation. We can build on the tendency to imitate by consciously asking students to imitate written models.

Read, Think, Summarize, and Interpret Strategy

When writers copy, it may simply mean that their understanding of the text is not yet complete. They may be unable to formulate their own response without the author's original words. Students may copy material inappropriately because they are not able to interpret the text independently. These students are not being intentionally deceptive. Struggling students often copy to gain insight into their personal understanding of the text. This may signal that they are not yet in control of their

Figure 17
Excerpt From Student Poem Created by Using the
"I Wish I Could Write Like That" Strategy

If I Were in Charge of the School

If I were in charge of the school
I'd cancel homework,
Early mornings,
And January.

If I were in charge of the school
There would be longer recesses,
Bigger desks,
Limousines home,
And an indoor McDonalds.

If I were in charge of the school
Every gym period would be basketball,
Every math period would be gym,
Every science period would be math,
Every social studies period would be
   gone.

If I were in charge of the school
A person whose grammar was not well,
And a person who could not spell,
Would still be allowed to be
In charge of the school.

own writing process and are in need of help from others to learn appropriate ways around the difficulty.

For students who do tend to copy verbatim from someone else's work, Collins (1998) offers the Read, Think, Summarize, and Interpret Strategy in which students fold one sheet of paper in half longways, forming two vertical columns. On the left side of the paper, students can write a summary of what they are reading; on the right side, they insert their responses and interpretations of the reading. This double-entry note taking encourages writers to summarize and interpret the main ideas and facts from a text and put these ideas into their own words.

Visualizing

We know that some struggling writers have trouble learning writing strategies through verbal channels, that is, through teacher talk and text-book language that describes writing techniques in exclusively linguistic terms (Collins & Collins, 1996). These writers may have learning strategies that are tuned into nonverbal channels rather than verbal ones. They may require visual ways of making writing manageable.

As a teacher of very young children, I have been aware of the connection between drawing and writing. Primary grade children almost always produce writing in connection with an illustration. In their writing, the words and illustrations are both descriptive. Together, words and illustrations provide insight into the details of the scene. Collins (1998) supports the notion that writers continue to rely on visualization throughout their school years and beyond, saying, "Images are synchronic, giving the whole picture at once, while language is diachronic, giving us meaning over time. Images therefore can help us see, quite literally, where our understanding of both topic and words is going" (p. 161). Visualization assists in the ability to solve writing problems. For teachers, this may mean providing opportunities for writers to experience visual strategies.

Visualization also can help writers organize their pieces. The ability to picture a sentence, a paragraph, or a text assists a writer in planning. Even strong writers resort to visualization to overcome writing hurdles. For example, I recently received an e-mail from a fellow graduate student requesting information about the format of a literature review for a master's thesis. My friend was trying to get a sense of the whole text. I believe she was searching for a graphic representation of the structure of a literature review. I was able to appeal to her visual learning by providing a picture of an inverted triangle, a picture my advisor once drew for me. This simplistic shape helped me organize my writing by graphically representing a beginning with a broad focus on the field of writing education. From this broad beginning, I could see how I needed to slowly become more specific as I finally focused narrowly on my thesis question.

Boxing Strategy

For struggling writers, who may not have a mental representation of what a finished piece should look like, a simple graphic representation such as the one in Figure 18 can create a mental image in the mind of the writer. This template can become a visual guide for organizing ideas

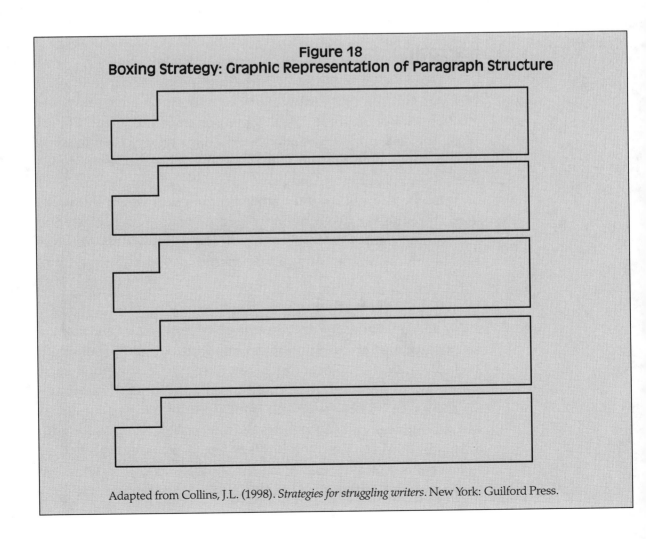

Figure 18
Boxing Strategy: Graphic Representation of Paragraph Structure

Adapted from Collins, J.L. (1998). *Strategies for struggling writers*. New York: Guilford Press.

into paragraphs. Young writers, who have not yet acquired an understanding of text structure intuitively from reading, can draw boxes in their piece of writing around the sentences that go together. With this visual aid, young writers can begin to group ideas together and understand indentation. Boxes drawn around each group of ideas can provide students with a visual image of what a finished piece might look like, and can help them build knowledge of writing structures. In an extension of this strategy, it is possible for students to learn about the importance of a topic sentence by underlining the major idea in each paragraph. This can contribute to content organization and can assist students in planning their writing. (See Collins, 1998.)

Narrating

Narrative writing, especially narratives of personal experience, are very popular in process-based writing classrooms, and narrating is the most popular of the three default strategies among teachers (Collins, 1998). The underlying assumption behind this strategy is that narrative writing comes more naturally than expository or persuasive writing because writers have a broad experience base with narration. Because much conversation and talk is in the narrative form, young writers have practiced narrating in spoken language long before they began to write. Therefore, students—especially those who struggle—are often encouraged to write stories based on past experiences.

Written Conversation

A written conversation can be an effective way to initiate and promote narrative writing. This narrating strategy simply provides an opportunity for students to "talk" to someone on paper. A teacher or other adult might initiate a written conversation by posing a question such as, "Can you tell me about your hockey team?" The student responds to this question in writing. When the student completes his or her response, the teacher poses a second question on paper that builds on what has already been written.

With this strategy, a teacher can carry on a conversation with a small group of students around a table. While one student is responding to a question, the teacher can initiate a note to a second child. As students grow comfortable with written conversation, they can begin to talk to one another in writing.

Journal Writing

Journal writing also allows for the development of narrative writing. In journals, students record daily thoughts, ideas, feelings, or events. Students can write about an after-school event, discuss an exciting movie, describe their athletic endeavors, or tell about a family trip. Through journal writing, students can explore topics that are personally meaningful. This form of narrative writing can promote fluency and exploration of new ideas.

Collins (1998) reminds us that "in teaching 'new' writing strategies, we should keep in mind the 'old' strategies students bring to the classroom" (p. 183). When writing becomes difficult, we can encourage students to use their default strategies as starting points for learning about writing.

References

Applebee, A., & Langer, J.A. (1983). Instructional scaffolding: Reading and writing as natural language activities. *Language Arts, 60*(2), 168–175.

Atwell, N. (1987). *In the middle: Writing, reading, and learning with adolescents.* Portsmouth, NH: Boynton/Cook.

Avery, C.S. (1987). Traci: A learning-disabled child in a writing-process classroom. In G.D. Bissex & R.H. Bullock (Eds.), *Seeing for ourselves: Case-study research by teachers of writing* (pp. 59–75). Portsmouth, NH: Heinemann.

Barenbaum, E.M., Newcomer, P.L., & Nodine, B.F. (1987). Children's ability to write stories as a function of variation in task, age, and developmental level. *Learning Disability Quarterly, 10,* 175–188.

Bartholomae, D. (1980). The study of error. *College Composition and Communications, 31,* 253–269.

Bear, D.R., Invernizzi, M., Templeton, S., & Johnston, F. (2000). *Words their way: Word study for phonics, vocabulary, and spelling instruction.* Englewood Cliffs, NJ: Prentice-Hall.

Bereiter, C., & Scardamalia, M. (1987). *The psychology of written composition.* Hillsdale, NJ: Erlbaum.

Berninger, V.W., Abbott, R.D., Whitaker, D., Sylvester, L., & Nolen, S. (1995). Integrating low- and high-level skills in instructional protocols for writing disabilities. *Learning Disability Quarterly, 18*(4), 293–309.

Borkowski, J.G. (1992). Metacognitive theory: A framework for teaching literacy, writing, and math skills. *Journal of Learning Disabilties, 25*(4), 253–257.

Bos, C.S., & Anders, P.L. (1990). Interactive teaching and learning: Instructional practices for teaching content and strategic knowledge. In T.E. Scruggs & B.Y.L. Wong (Eds.), *Intervention research in learning disabilities* (pp. 166–185). New York: Springer-Verlag.

Bruner, J.S. (1986). *Actual minds, possible worlds.* Cambridge, MA: Harvard University Press.

Calkins, L.M. (1983). *Lessons from a child: On the teaching and learning of writing.* Portsmouth, NH: Heinemann.

Calkins, L.M. (1994). *The art of teaching writing.* Portsmouth, NH: Heinemann.

Cambourne, B. (1995). Toward an educationally relevant theory of literacy learning: Twenty years of inquiry. *The Reading Teacher, 49,* 182–190.

Cason, N. (1991). Improving writing of at risk students with a focus on the African American male. *Bread Loaf News, 5*(2), 26–29. (ED 404 637)

Christophel, D.M. (1990). The relationship among teacher immediacy behaviors, student motivation, and learning. *Communication Education, 39*, 323–340.

Cleary, L.M. (1991). *From the other side of the desk: Students speak out about writing.* Portsmouth, NH: Boynton/Cook.

Collins, J.L. (1998). *Strategies for struggling writers.* New York: Guilford.

Collins, K.M., & Collins, J.L. (1996). Strategic instruction for struggling writers. *English Journal, 85*(6), 54–61.

Cunningham, P.M. (2000). *Phonics they use: Words for reading and writing.* New York: Longman.

Danoff, B., Harris, K.R., & Graham, S. (1993). Incorporating strategy instruction within the writing process in the regular classroom: Effects on the students with and without learning disabilities. *Journal of Reading Behaviour, 25*(3), 295–322.

Delpit, L.D. (1988). The silenced dialogue: Power and pedagogy in educating other people's children. *Harvard Educational Review, 58*, 280–298.

Dillon, D.R. (2000). *Kids insight: Reconsidering how to meet the literacy needs of all students.* Newark, DE: International Reading Association.

Dixon-Krauss, L. (1996). *Vygotsky in the classroom: Mediated literacy instruction and assessment.* White Plains, NY: Longman.

DuCharme, C., Earl, J., & Poplin, M.S. (1989). The author model: The constructivist view of the writing process. *Learning Disability Quarterly,12*, 237–242.

Dwyer, E.J., & Dwyer, E.E. (1994). How teacher attitudes influence reading achievement. In E.H. Cramer & M. Castle (Eds.), *Fostering the love of reading: The affective domain in reading education* (pp. 66–73). Newark, DE: International Reading Association.

Dyson, A.H. (1990). Talking up a writing community: The role of talk in learning to write. In S. Hynds & D.L. Rubin (Eds.), *Perspectives on talk and learning* (pp. 99–114). Urbana, IL: National Council of Teachers of English.

Emig, J. (1971). *The composing processes of twelfth graders.* Urbana, IL: National Council of Teachers of English.

Englert, C.S. (1990). Writing through strategy instruction. In T.E. Scruggs & B.Y.L. Wong (Eds.), *Intervention research in learning disabilities* (pp. 186–223). New York: Springer-Verlag.

Englert, C.S., & Mariage, T.V. (1991). Shared understandings: Structuring the writing experience through dialogue. *Journal of Learning Disabilities, 24*(6), 330–342.

Englert, C.S., & Raphael, T.E. (1989). Developing successful writers through cognitive strategy instruction. In J.E. Brophy (Ed.), *Advances in research on teaching* (Vol. 1, pp. 105–151). Greenwich, CT: JAI Press.

Englert, C.S., Raphael, T.E., Anderson, L.M., Anthony, H.M., & Stevens, D.D. (1991). Making strategies and self-talk visible: Writing instruction in regular and special education classrooms. *American Educational Research Journal, 28*, 337–372.

Englert, C.S., Raphael, T.E. , Anderson, L.M., Gregg, S., & Anthony, H.M. (1989). Exposition: Reading, writing, and metacognitive knowledge of learning disabled students. *Learning Disabilities Research, 5,* 5–24.

Englert, C.S., Raphael, T.E., Fear, K.L., & Anderson, L.M. (1988). Students' metacognitive knowledge about how to write informational texts. *Learning Disabilities Quarterly, 11,* 18–46.

Fletcher, R. (1996). *Breathing in, breathing out: Keeping a writer's notebook.* Portsmouth, NH: Heinemann.

Flower, L. (1981). *Problem-solving strategies for writing.* New York: Harcourt Brace Jovanovich.

Freedman, S.W. (1987). *Response to student writing.* Urbana, IL: National Council of Teachers of English.

Gagne, E.D. (1985). *The cognitive psychology of school learning.* Boston: Little, Brown.

Ganske, K. (2000). *Word journeys: Assessment-guided phonics, spelling, and vocabulary instruction.* New York: Guilford.

Gere, A.R. (1990). Talking in writing groups. In S. Hynds & D.L. Rubin (Eds.), *Perspectives on talk and learning* (pp. 115–128). Urbana, IL: National Council of Teachers of English.

Glesne, C., & Peshkin, A. (1992). *Becoming qualitative researchers: An introduction.* New York: Longman.

Good T.L., & Brophy, J. (1987). *Looking in classrooms* (4th ed.). New York: Harper-Collins.

Graham, S. (1990). The role of production factors in learning disabled students' compositions. *Journal of Educational Psychology, 82*(4), 781–791.

Graham, S. (1992). Helping students with LD progress as writers. *Intervention in School and Clinic, 27*(3), 134–144.

Graham, S., & Harris, K.R. (1988). Instructional recommendations for teaching writing to exceptional students. *Exceptional Children, 54,* 506–512.

Graham, S., & Harris, K.R. (1989). Components analysis of cognitive strategy instruction: Effects of learning disabled students' compositions and self-efficacy. *Journal of Educational Psychology, 81,* 353–361.

Graham, S., & Harris, K.R. (1994). Implications of constructivism for teaching writing to students with special needs. *The Journal of Special Education, 28*(3), 275–289.

Graham, S., Schwartz, S., & MacArthur, C.A. (1993). Knowledge of writing and the composing process, attitude toward writing, and self-efficacy for students with and without learning disabilities. *Journal of Learning Disabilities, 26*(4), 237–249.

Graves, D.H. (1983). *Writing: Teachers and children at work.* Portsmouth, NH: Heinemann.

Graves, D.H. (1985). All children can write. *Learning Disabilities Focus, 1,* 36–43.

Graves, D.H. (1991). All children can write. In S. Stires (Ed.), *With promise: Redefining reading and writing for "special" students* (pp. 115–126). Portsmouth, NH: Heinemann.

Graves, D.H. (1994). *A fresh look at writing.* Portsmouth, NH: Heinemann.

Greenfield, P.M. (1984). A theory of the teacher in the learning activities of everyday life. In B. Rogoff & J. Lave (Eds.), *Everyday cognition: Its development in social context* (pp. 117–138). Cambridge, MA: Harvard University Press.

Guthrie, J.T., & Wigfield, A. (1997). *Reading engagement: Motivating readers through integrated instruction.* Newark, DE: International Reading Association.

Hairston, M. (1982). The winds of change: Thomas Kuhn and the revolution in the teaching of writing. *College Composition and Communication, 33,* 76–88.

Harris, K.R., & Graham, S. (1992). *Helping young writers master the craft: Strategy instruction and self-regulation in the writing process.* Cambridge, MA: Brookline.

Harris, K.R., & Graham, S. (1996a). *Making the writing process work: Strategies for composition and self-regulation.* Cambridge, MA: Brookline.

Harris, K.R., & Graham, S. (1996b). Memo to constructivists: Skills count, too. *Educational Leadership, 53,* 26–29.

Harris, K.R., & Pressley, M. (1991). The nature of cognitive strategy instruction: Interactive strategy construction. *Exceptional Children, 57,* 392–405.

Harris, M. (1990). Teacher/student talk: The collaborative conference. In S. Hynds & D.L. Rubin (Eds.), *Perspectives on talk and learning* (pp. 149–161). Urbana, IL: National Council of Teachers of English.

Harste, J. (1990). Jerry Harste speaks on reading and writing. *The Reading Teacher, 43,* 316–317.

Heathington, B.S. (1994). Affect versus skills: Choices for teachers. In E.H. Cramer & M. Castle (Eds.), *Fostering the love of reading: The affective domain in reading education* (pp. 199–208). Newark, DE: International Reading Association.

John-Steiner, V. (1985). *Notebooks of the mind: Explorations of thinking.* Albuquerque, NM: University of New Mexico Press.

Keefe, C.H. (1996). *Label-free learning.* York, ME: Stenhouse.

Lamott, A. (1994). *Bird by bird: Some instructions on writing and life.* New York: Pantheon.

Lensmire, T.J. (1994a). *When children write: Critical re-visions of the writing workshop.* New York: Teachers College Press.

Lensmire, T.J. (1994b). Writing workshop as carnival: Reflections on an alternative learning environment. *Harvard Educational Review, 64*(4), 371–391.

Lensmire, T.J. (1997). *Powerful writing, responsible teaching.* New York: Teachers College Press.

MacArthur, C., & Graham, S. (1987). Learning disabled students' composing under three methods of text production: Handwriting, word processing, and dictation. *Journal of Special Education, 21*(3), 22–42.

MacArthur, C.A., Graham, S., & Schwartz, S. (1991). Knowledge of revision and revising behavior among students with learning disabilities. *Learning Disability Quarterly, 14,* 61–73.

MacArthur, C.A., Schwartz, S., & Graham, S. (1991). A model for writing instruction: Integrating word processing and strategy instruction into a process approach to writing. *Learning Disabilities Research and Practice, 6*(4), 230–236.

Mather, N. (1992). Whole language reading instruction for students with learning disabilities: Caught in the cross fire. *Learning Disabilities Research and Practice, 7,* 87–95.

McIver, M.C., & Wolf, S.A. (1999). The power of the conference *is* the power of suggestion. *Language Arts, 77*(1), 54–61.

Montague, M., Maddux, C., & Dereshiwsky, M. (1990). Story grammar and comprehension and production of narrative prose by students with learning disabilities. *Journal of Learning Disabilities, 23*(3), 190–197.

Moran, M. (1981). Performance of learning disabled and low achieving secondary students on formal features of paragraph-writing task. *Learning Disability Quarterly, 4,* 271–280.

Morocco, C.C., & Newman, S.B. (1986). Word processors and the acquisition of writing strategies. *Journal of Learning Disabilities, 19*(4), 243–247.

Morris, N., & Crump, W.D. (1982). Syntactic and vocabulary development in the written language of learning disabled and non-learning disabled students at four age levels. *Learning Disability Quarterly, 5,* 163–172.

Murray, D.M. (1984). *Write to learn.* New York: Holt, Rinehart and Winston.

Murray, D.M. (1996). *Write to learn* (5th ed.). Fort Worth, TX: Harcourt Brace.

Newcomer, P.L., & Barenbaum, E.M. (1991). The written composing ability of children with learning disabilities: A review of the literature from 1980 to 1990. *Journal of Learning Disabilities, 24*(10), 578–593.

Nodine, B.F., Barenbaum, E.M., & Newcomer, P.L. (1985). Story composition by learning disabled, reading disabled, and normal children. *Learning Disability Quarterly, 8,* 167–179.

Odden, A. (1987). School effectiveness, backward mapping, and state education policies. In J. Lane & H. Walbert (Eds.), *Effective school leadership* (pp. 33–59). Berkeley, CA: McCutchan.

Palincsar, A.S. (1986a). Metacognitive strategy instruction. *Exceptional Children, 53*(2), 118–124.

Palincsar, A.S. (1986b). The role of dialogue in providing scaffolded instruction. *Educational Psychologist, 21,* 73–98.

Poplin, M.S. (1988). Holistic/constructivist principles of the teaching/learning process: Implication for the field of learning disabilities. *Journal of Learning Disabilities, 21,* 401–406.

Power, B., & Ohanian, S. (1999). Sacred cows: Questioning assumptions in elementary writing programs. *Language Arts, 76*(3), 249–257.

Pressley, M., & Levin, J. (1986). Elaborative learning strategies for the inefficient learner. In S. Ceci (Ed.), *Handbook of cognitive, social, and neuropsychological aspects of learning disabilities* (pp. 175–211). Hillsdale, NJ: Erlbaum.

Pressley, M., & Woloshyn, V. (1995). *Cognitive strategy instruction that really improves children's academic performance.* Cambridge, MA: Brookline.

Robeck, M.C., & Wallace, R.R. (1990). *The psychology of reading: An interdisciplinary approach* (2nd ed.). Hillsdale, NJ: Erlbaum.

Rogoff, B., & Gardner, W. (1984). Adult guidance of cognitive development. In B. Rogoff & J. Lave (Eds.), *Everyday cognition: Its development in social context* (pp. 95–116). Cambridge, MA: Harvard University Press.

Rogoff, B., & Lave, J. (1984). *Everyday cognition: Its development in social context*. Cambridge, MA: Harvard University Press.

Roller, C.M. (1996). *Variability not disability: Struggling readers in a workshop classroom*. Newark, DE: International Reading Association.

Rose, M. (1989). *Lives on the boundary: The struggles and achievements of America's underprepared*. New York: Free Press.

Scheid, K. (1991). *Effective writing instruction for students with learning problems: The instructional methods report series*. Columbus, OH: Information Center for Special Education Media and Materials. (ED 340 177)

Seuss, Dr., Prelutsky, J., & Smith, L. (1998). *Hooray for diffendoofer day!* New York: Knopf.

Shaughnessy, M.P. (1977). *Errors and expectations: A guide for the teaching of basic writing*. New York: Oxford University Press.

Smith, F. (1988). *Joining the literacy club*. Portsmouth, NH: Heinemann.

Spiegel, D.L. (1992). Blending whole language and systematic direct instruction. *The Reading Teacher, 46*, 38–44.

Spiegel, D.L., (1994). A portrait of parents of successful readers. In E.H. Cramer & M. Castle (Eds.), *Fostering the love of reading: The affective domain in reading education* (pp. 74–87). Newark, DE: International Reading Association.

Swanson, L. (1989). Strategy instruction: Overview of principles and procedures for effective use. *Learning Disability Quarterly, 12*, 3–15.

Thomas, C.C., Englert, C.S., & Gregg, S. (1987). An analysis of errors and strategies in the expository writing of learning disabled students. *Remedial and Special Education, 8*(1), 21–30.

Vallecorsa, A., & Garriss, C. (1990). Story composition skills of middle-grade students with learning disabilities. *Exceptional Children, 57*, 48–53.

Viorst, J. (1981). *If I were in charge of the world and other worries*. New York: Atheneum.

Vygotsky, L.S. (1978). *Mind in society: The development of higher psychological processes* (M. Cole, V. John-Steiner, S. Scribner, & E. Souberman, Eds. & Trans.). Cambridge, MA: Harvard University Press. (Original work published 1934)

Wells, G., & Chang-Wells, G.L. (1992). *Constructing knowledge together: Classrooms as centers of inquiry and literacy*. Portsmouth, NH: Heinemann.

Wilkinson, L.C. (1984). Peer group talk in elementary school. *Language Arts, 61*(2), 164–169.

Index

Page references followed by *b* or *f* indicate boxes or figures, respectively.

JOURNAL, 2. *See also* teacher's log; writing notebook
JOURNALING, 57*b*; as writing strategy, 150–151

K

KEEFE, C.H., 37
KENDA: encouragement for, 106; final draft by, 60*f*; frustrations of, 1, 97–98; growth of, 117; initial observation of, 18–24; introduction to, 3; peer-edited story by, 22*f*–23*f*; perceptions of writing, 93–94; poem by, 19*f*; scaffolding for, 57–63; strategies constructed by, 75*f*

L

LAMOTT, A., 104
LANGER, J.A., 15
LAVE, J., 47
LEARNING: Christenson on, 15–16; collaborative, 110–111; conditions for, 68–70, 69*f*; Reflection Points on, 96; from struggling writers, 1–16, 90–115, 125–127; Vygotsky on, resources on, 102*b*
LENSMIRE, T.J., 77, 78*b*, 101, 121
LEVIN, J., 18, 44, 46
LITERACY: conditions for learning and, 68–70, 69*f*

M

MACARTHUR, C.A., 14, 34, 42*b*, 46, 77–78, 93, 108*b*, 122
MADDUX, C., 32
MANNING, B.H., 84*b*
MARIAGE, T.V., 101, 116
MATHER, N., 76, 121, 126
MCIVER, M.C., 103
MECHANICS OF WRITING, 19–20; scaffolding for, 63–66; of struggling writers, 33
METACOGNITIVE KNOWLEDGE, 44–47; Reflection Points on, 47; resources on, 46*b*; types of, 45
MODELING, 109; cognitive processes, 84–87; self-talk, 71; writing conferencing, 102–104
MOLLOY, D., 42*b*
MONTAGUE, M., 32
MORAN, M., 33
MOROCCO, C.C., 35
MORRIS, N., 33
MOTIVATION FOR WRITING, 24–25; encouragement and, 106–107; scaffolding for, 67–73; self-monitoring on, 143
MURRAY, D., 1, 11*b*, 40, 121